Making Meaning of Difficult Experiences

Making Meaning of Difficult Experiences

A SELF-GUIDED PROGRAM

Sheila A.M. Rauch, PhD
and Barbara Olasov Rothbaum, PhD

OXFORD
UNIVERSITY PRESS

OXFORD
UNIVERSITY PRESS

Oxford University Press is a department of the University of Oxford. It furthers
the University's objective of excellence in research, scholarship, and education
by publishing worldwide. Oxford is a registered trade mark of Oxford University
Press in the UK and certain other countries.

Published in the United States of America by Oxford University Press
198 Madison Avenue, New York, NY 10016, United States of America.

Library of Congress Cataloging-in-Publication Data
Names: Rauch, Sheila A. M., author. | Rothbaum, Barbara Olasov, author.
Title: Making meaning of difficult experiences : a self-guided program /
Sheila A.M. Rauch, and Barbara Olasov Rothbaum.
Description: New York, NY : Oxford University Press, [2023] |
Includes bibliographical references and index. |
Identifiers: LCCN 2023004657 (print) | LCCN 2023004658 (ebook) |
ISBN 9780197642573 (paperback) | ISBN 9780197642597 (epub) | ISBN 9780197642603
Subjects: LCSH: Post-traumatic stress disorder. | Psychic trauma—Treatment. |
Life change events. | Adjustment (Psychology)
Classification: LCC RC552.P67 R3828 2023 (print) | LCC RC552.P67 (ebook) |
DDC 616.85/21—dc23/eng/20230526
LC record available at https://lccn.loc.gov/2023004657
LC ebook record available at https://lccn.loc.gov/2023004658

DOI: 10.1093/med-psych/9780197642573.001.0001

Printed by Sheridan Books, Inc., United States of America

CONTENTS

Preface   vii
Author Note   ix

Introduction   1

Chapter 1: Traumatic Experiences   5

Chapter 2: Why Approach Difficult Experiences?   13

Chapter 3: How to Approach Difficult Experiences: Memory Exposure
and Processing   25

Chapter 4: Getting Active   61

Chapter 5: The Healing Power of Social Connection   75

Chapter 6: Self-Care   85

Chapter 7: Closing the Book on Difficult Experiences   105

Appendix A: Worksheets   117
Appendix B: Suggestions for Pleasant Activities   187
Appendix C: Additional Resources   191
Index   199

PREFACE

Why did we write a book to help people process their difficult experiences? Unfortunately, we live in a sometimes dangerous and stressful world. Most of us will move through difficult experiences, possibly changed but generally unscathed. But some of us will not, and some experiences will change us forever. We are still experiencing a pandemic that has left no one untouched and which seems to have amplified every experience as our worlds have become narrower. The best way to process difficult experiences is by talking about them with supportive people, but the pandemic has limited social contact in person and therefore changed some of the usual ways we get support from others.

As the authors of this workbook, over the past few decades we have worked with many people to process difficult and traumatic experiences and have seen their lives positively transformed. Many of our clients have told us that after processing the memories of their difficult experiences, they feel like the people they were before the experience happened, and they hadn't thought that this would be possible. We know that the skills described in this book work, so we wanted to share them more widely.

So that is why we have written a workbook to process difficult experiences! We want to help people move through to the other side of experiences that can derail a life. We want to let everyone learn these skills that have worked for our clients and thousands (maybe millions at this point) of others. We want *you* to live the life that *you* want to live.

We owe a debt of gratitude to all our clients and the many therapists we've trained. We have learned from every single one of you. Thank you. This is our way of paying it forward.

AUTHOR NOTE

Together we have more than 50 years of combined clinical and research experience helping survivors of trauma and stressful life experiences. The case examples found in *Making Meaning of Difficult Experiences: A Self-Guided Program* are all fictional people, based on our experience and examples of real client situations, but they are not reflective of any specific people we have seen in practice. This is to ensure the privacy of our clients.

Introduction

We live in a dangerous and stressful world, but without adversity, there is no resilience. *Making Meaning of Difficult Experiences: A Self-Guided Program* is a self-help workbook created to help people deal with the difficult experiences that life inevitably brings and emerge resilient. This includes all that we have experienced since the beginning of the COVID-19 pandemic, as well as the other stressful and traumatic experiences many of us will face at least once, such as death of a loved one, job loss, divorce, sexual harassment, sexual or physical assault, serious illness, natural disasters, car crashes, gender- or race-based trauma, and/or microaggressions.

Unfortunately, the list goes on. *Making Meaning of Difficult Experiences* is meant to help us get back to our lives following stressful and traumatic situations, including post-pandemic life. This workbook has tools and strategies for everyone—for those people who have had difficult and potentially traumatic experiences and who wish to work through them, as well as for people who have not had specific difficult experiences but who want to be ready to move forward as we work to put traumatic events behind us. The pandemic has left no one untouched. Even the hardiest of us are burnt out at the very least. Most are bruised. Many are scarred and will be changed forever.

While *Making Meaning of Difficult Experiences* is not just a pandemic recovery tool, the pandemic is really what pushed us to create this self-help resource. Knowing that the mental healthcare system even prior to COVID could not care for all those dealing with high levels of stress and trauma, we wanted to provide a new resource for people to use on their own (without a therapist or counselor) to approach these experiences and the memories they left behind and to move through them to the other side.

As of this writing in early 2023, countless people the world over are grappling with extreme emotional distress as a result of the COVID-19 pandemic, millions have died globally, and more than one million have died in the United States. Struggles that may arise as the result of these experiences include

- having cared for the dying
- witnessing death and dying, with the associated fear of exposure to and infection by the virus
- sudden unexpected loss of loved ones
- hospitalization, particularly with life-threatening illness
- sudden financial instability and/or job loss
- extreme social isolation
- domestic violence intensified by stay-at-home orders
- other highly distressing experiences that are persistently troubling

Everyone has been affected by this pandemic. Those most heavily affected include physicians, nurses, and other healthcare workers; essential workers daily exposed to dangerous situations such as transporting symptomatic people and working in crowded retail settings; and anyone bereaved by the loss of someone close.

Traumatic experiences are certainly not limited to those surrounding the pandemic. Increased awareness and incidents of racial, ethnic, religious, gender-based trauma, and trauma directed at those in the LGBTQ community have also increased and impacted many. Indeed, up to 90% of US adults will experience one or more potentially traumatic events in their lifetimes, including

- interpersonal violence
- traffic collision or other life-threatening accident
- hate crimes and racial/ethnic violence
- sexual assault
- natural disasters
- combat or other military trauma

Making Meaning of Difficult Experiences is for them, too, and can also help with more common but still tragic life events such as the death of a loved one, miscarriage, and divorce.

We invite you to read through our workbook, engage with the exercises and worksheets, learn from our sample stories and illustrations, and emerge on the other side of your difficult experiences. For all memory processing activities in this workbook, you can choose to complete the printed worksheets in the chapters or you may choose to audio-record the memory using the Messy Memories app, available from the Apple App Store or Google Play. The printed worksheets also appear all together near the end of this workbook in Appendix A: Worksheets, and they can be accessed by searching for this book's title on the Oxford Academic platform at academic.oup .com. We expect that most people who pick up the workbook will see benefits in about 2–4 weeks if they are working daily on the exercises; results may take longer (6–8 weeks) if they are working only a few times per week. Some people may begin to see benefit after their first time processing a difficult experience. For others, it may take more time. Everyone is different, and their difficult experiences vary as well. Appendix A includes enough worksheets for 6 weeks of work. More are available online if it takes longer or if you want to use this workbook again in the future, and you should always feel free to copy worksheets and add sheets of paper. This is your experience—make it your own to get as much out of it as you can.

CHAPTER 1

Traumatic Experiences

TRAUMATIC EXPERIENCES: GETTING STUCK AND UNSTUCK

Traumatic events and other difficult experiences can have long-lasting effects on mental health and well-being. While most people who suffer a trauma naturally recover over time, for others mental health difficulties continue and may trigger full-blown depression, posttraumatic stress disorder (PTSD), substance use disorders, anxiety disorders, and/or other problems that interfere with healthy daily functioning. Individuals may become "stuck" in the memory of the trauma and may report feeling haunted by it. This feeling of being trapped by the experience then leads many people to avoid thinking and talking about it and to avoid situations, people, or places that remind them of it. This can have a disastrous effect on daily life and mental health.

Many years of research (much of which has been conducted by the authors of this book) have shown that people who try to avoid memories and reminders of difficult experiences are *more likely* to report PTSD, depression, and other problems in the long term. Many mental health providers describe this phenomenon with the example of the "pink elephant." It may sound familiar. The idea is that if I ask you to think of anything except a pink elephant, of course the only thing you *can* think of is a pink elephant. Difficult memories can be like that pink elephant—the more you try to not think about them, the more often and intensely they come to mind. On the other hand, those who work to emotionally process (work through) a traumatic memory—rather than avoiding or repressing it—gradually regain a general sense of well-being and tend to fare better over time.

The saying "time heals all wounds" is only partially true. For those who emotionally process what happened and gradually approach and reengage in life, time does heal; but for those who avoid, time typically compounds suffering, and problems get worse (not to worry: we'll explain later exactly what we mean by "emotionally process"). If you are interested in more in-depth information on the impact of trauma and PTSD and effective treatments, our book *PTSD: What Everyone Needs to Know* provides a concise review of what we know about this common and impactful mental health issue in an easy-to-read format, and we have some similar content in this workbook. That said, you should also know that a person does not need a formal diagnosis of PTSD to be severely troubled by a traumatic event, and this book may help you move past that event even if you do not have PTSD. The same concepts apply to processing other difficult experiences.

WHAT DO DIFFICULT EXPERIENCES LOOK LIKE?

Throughout *Making Meaning of Difficult Experiences: A Self-Guided Program*, we illustrate key points using brief stories of people who have undergone traumatic or other difficult experiences. These are not real people, but their stories include elements from different people we have worked with over the years. The following are examples of different difficult experiences.

INTRODUCING OUR CASE EXAMPLES

Ann

Ann had a tough week at work and wanted to unwind. She went out to a club on her own since none of her friends was available. After an hour of dancing, she got a drink from the bar and quickly began to feel very drunk and unsteady. She went to the restroom and did not notice that a man followed her in. She continued to feel worse as she walked to the bathroom stall. The stall was spinning, and she was seeing spots as a man pushed open the stall door, pushed Ann into the stall ahead of him, and slammed the door shut behind them. Ann was losing consciousness as the man grabbed her head and pushed her up against the wall. Ann lost consciousness, and he raped her in the bathroom stall. The next thing Ann remembered was stumbling out of the stall in a lot of pain. She had been sexually assaulted and had no idea who had assaulted her. She limped out of the bathroom and could only clumsily move her arms and legs. Another woman saw her and ran over to ask if she was okay. Ann told her that she was not feeling well and that she lived just round the corner. The stranger said she would help her walk home.

David

David is an ICU nurse who cared for COVID-19 patients during the pandemic. He had to make decisions about who would get what help when supplies were low, and he held too many hands of dying patients when their families were not allowed to be with them. His colleagues were getting sick, and the hospital was low on staff for every shift. David was so exhausted that he stopped exercising, wasn't eating properly, and was socially isolated. During his little time off, he was drinking too much and not sleeping. There was so much to be done and so many to be helped, and David felt that he was in a downward spiral. While there were lots of upsetting experiences he endured during the pandemic, the loss of a patient named Clem was particularly difficult, and he often had nightmares about this death even several months later.

Helen

Helen's car was hit by an 18-wheeler on her way to work in rainy rush-hour traffic. She was hit, spun around, lost consciousness, and woke up in the ambulance on the way to the hospital. After the crash, she talked over and over to her family and friends and anyone who would listen about what happened during and after the crash and how she was terrified she would be killed. She made herself drive again as soon as she was able. Although this will always be a scary memory for her, Helen worked through it. She did what she knew she needed to do even when it made her think about the crash, and this is what helped her to work through it. As a result, she didn't have any lasting emotional problems from this car crash, and, within about 6 months, she was back to her life and rarely thought about the crash.

Miguel

Miguel was on his first deployment to Iraq and was driving back to base when he ran over an improvised explosive device (IED) that blew up his Humvee. The blast disoriented him and knocked out his hearing for at least a few minutes; he had loud ringing in his ears for hours more. His vehicle filled with smoke, and he smelled burning flesh. By the time he could respond, he understood that his vehicle was on fire, and he worked to open his door and get out. Miguel fell to the ground as he exited his vehicle, and he realized that his right leg was badly injured and bleeding.

His thoughts turned immediately to the three other soldiers in the vehicle, and he went to check on them. He opened the back door and helped pull out Horwitz, who had been sitting right behind him. Horwitz was conscious but stunned and appeared to be injured but possibly not seriously. The two of them moved as fast as they could to the other side of the vehicle to try to extract their two comrades from the front and back seats. The vehicle was in flames at this point. Soldiers from the Humvee behind theirs were already trying to extract the other two soldiers from Miguel's vehicle. Brown, in the backseat, was badly injured and burned, but she survived; Miguel's friend, Russo, in the front seat, did not.

Miguel tried to help the medic attending to Russo, but the medic told Miguel to lie down because he was injured. Miguel was air-lifted to the hospital, and, when stable, he was flown back to the United States for continued care. His leg was too badly injured to return to Iraq, and he was medically discharged from the Army.

Shaquila

Shaquila and Tanja were so excited when they got the news that she was pregnant. It was a long process to save the money for in vitro fertilization (IVF) and then an emotional process to go through the medical procedures. Both Shaquila and Tanja were looking forward to parenthood and excited to grow their family. Shaquila was doing well and was approaching 8 weeks into the pregnancy. They had just started telling people who were closest to them and planning for the baby's room. Monday morning, Shaquila started feeling abdominal pain and cramping and was bleeding. She was scared and called the doctor who told her to come in. They rushed to the doctor, but by the time they arrived, they both knew it was not going to be good news. The doctor saw her right away and confirmed that she was having a miscarriage. There was not a medical recourse to prevent it at this point. Both Shaquila and Tanja felt devastated. They knew they could try another course, but the financial and emotional impact of the last one meant they needed to wait. Shaquila fell into a sense of isolation and loss and was not able to get up to go work and didn't even care about eating. She returned to work after 2 weeks but felt like she was going through the motions. Tanja worried about Shaquila as the depression seemed to take over and she seemed to be stuck in a bad place.

These are examples of difficult experiences that can have very different impacts on people, depending on the person, the situation, and how they deal with it. Impacts will differ based on the event itself as well as on how the person who endured the situation thinks about the event and manages its aftermath. We will revisit these cases and others throughout *Making Meaning of Difficult Experiences* in order to highlight (1) how people vary in response and (2) how what people do to work through to the other side of difficult experiences safely and healthfully can lead to a more fulfilling life and a better sense of well-being.

HOW THIS BOOK CAN HELP YOU RECOVER FROM YOUR OWN DIFFICULT EXPERIENCES

While not a treatment itself, *Making Meaning of Difficult Experiences* is based on psychological treatments that have been studied extensively and proven effective. We have spent a combined 50 years helping people recover from life's worst moments, and we know what works. This workbook will walk you through several useful skills to help you process difficult and potentially traumatic events, with the goal of helping you avoid becoming "stuck" by the experience and unable to move on. This program is unique in that it is intended to be wholly self-directed, meaning that you can do it on your own, without a therapist. You can learn about and then immediately practice the skills described, moving through and then past difficult experiences—whether the experience happened last week or years ago. The program takes you step by step through four skills that facilitate the emotional processing of difficult experiences and getting back on track.

The four skills covered in this workbook are

- Skill 1: Memory Exposure and Processing (see Chapter 3 of this workbook)
- Skill 2: Getting Active (see Chapter 4 of this workbook)
- Skill 3: Social Connection (see Chapter 5 of this workbook)
- Skill 4: Self-Care (see Chapter 6 of this workbook)

In addition to this workbook, which will help you to work through the skills we'll shortly describe, you can also download the Messy Memories app we have created from the Apple App Store or Google Play if you prefer to use the app to guide you through memory exposure and processing and track your progress.

Skill 1: Memory Exposure and Processing (Chapter 3)

The only way to the other side of the pain is through it. When very stressful things happen, we need to think about them and their meaning—what these events tell us about ourselves and how they impact the way we see the world. This is what we mean by *processing*. If we don't process these experiences, we risk becoming stuck in them, which can lead to difficult and intense emotions like sadness, fear, or anger. Many people respond to a stressful memory that just won't go away by consciously trying to *push it out* of their minds, avoiding the memory or even people, places, or situations that remind them of the stressful event. The problem with avoidance is that the relief of trying not to think about something does not last; the memory returns despite our best efforts to not think about it. Skill 1 teaches you how to approach stressful memories in a way that allows you to move through the experience, feel the emotions that you have about it in a manageable way, and then move on. This is processing the memory. As you find a place for these stressful memories within your much broader and richer life story, and as the emotions connected to the memories become less intense, you will be better able to move on with life without the experiences haunting you. In Chapter 3, we will walk you through the memory processing steps that will help you get to the other side of these experiences.

Skill 2: Getting Active (Chapter 4)

Getting active is what we call our *behavioral activation* work. Behavioral activation is a powerful tool that helps people who are going through difficult experiences continue (or restart) doing things that they enjoy—even when distressed. Most of us neglect the hobbies and activities we love when we get very stressed and busy, so much so that we might not want to pursue them any more at all. But when we take the time to reengage in and enjoy them, research shows that we become more productive, more effective, and happier. In Chapter 4, we will help you to plan positive activities that are both reinforcing and sustainable over time.

Skill 3: Social Connection (Chapter 5)

Social support is one of the best ways to get through life's hardest moments. Unfortunately, when people are stressed, they sometimes avoid others and isolate themselves—and, of course, the social distancing required during the COVID-19 pandemic made things so much worse. For some, the process of getting back out in the world after being isolated at home in the pandemic is stressful and difficult. Avoiding people is especially common when we feel guilty or worried that others may blame us for part or all of what happened. No one likes to be judged, but sometimes survivors of difficult experiences are their own harshest judges, and they cannot benefit from the support of others unless they talk about what they've gone through. Chapter 5 focuses on having enough and the right kinds of social contacts to feel supported as you deal with stressful memories. Everyone is different as far as how much social connection they need and what types of connections work best for them. This part of the workbook will help you get more socially connected as you work through your experiences.

Skill 4: Self-Care (Chapter 6)

Many people have trouble prioritizing self-care when under stress. When there is too much to do, it can be hard to take the time to eat properly, sleep enough, or exercise. Chapter 6 focuses on what you usually do for self-care so that you can continue to use what has worked for you in the past. In addition, the chapter will help you think about new sources of self-care to try. Some people exercise, pray, or meditate. Others do crossword puzzles, play an instrument, or listen to music or dance. This chapter will help you practice and get into a habit of good self-care skills including getting enough sleep, eating properly, exercising, and making sure you continue to pursue activities and social connections that make you happy.

HOW TO USE THIS WORKBOOK

Each of the skill chapters in this workbook begins with a look at one or more of our case study examples followed by an in-depth discussion of the skill covered in the chapter as well as worksheets for you to complete. You can use the worksheets to figure out what is working or not working for you and to consider how to focus your time on the skills to meet your needs. This may mean spending more time on one skill or equal time across the skills, making use of the complete program. You get to choose what you want to work on and where you feel like you're good.

We suggest you start with the memory exposure and processing skill described in Chapter 3, and use the worksheets in this book or the app (or both). *One helpful hint: the skills that you really don't want to practice might be the ones you need the most!*

In order for you to check on your progress, please make sure to complete the worksheets in the book or in the app, which will be asking you questions about how you are feeling periodically and after certain exercises.

WHEN IS *MAKING MEANING OF DIFFICULT EXPERIENCES* NOT ENOUGH?

If you would like to reach out to a mental health professional at any time while using this workbook, please don't hesitate to do so. This is not a resource that you have to use alone, and we recommend that you take advantage of your available supports as much as you are able. In addition, if you see that things are not getting better (for example, your sleep is getting worse, you're more angry or are lashing out more at others, you're unable to get out of bed or are unmotivated to get things done during the day) even after using the skills for a few weeks, it may make sense to seek mental health resources and get some assistance. Effective treatments are available that can include medication, psychotherapy, and even some combinations of these strategies. (We review PTSD and effective treatments in our book *PTSD: What Everyone Needs to Know*, in case you're interested in learning more.) If at any time you feel you would like to speak with a professional, you can call your employee assistance program (sometimes referred to as EAP) if you are employed outside of the home or call your state mental health or psychological association to help connect you with a provider. In Chapter 7, "Closing the Book on Difficult Experiences," we provide direction on when additional help may be needed as well as how to access that assistance. In addition, in Appendix C, "Additional Resources," near the end of this workbook, we provide information on some additional mental health resources you may be able to access.

> If you are having thoughts about harming yourself or someone else, please call 911 for immediate assistance, go to your nearest emergency room, or contact the National Suicide Prevention Lifeline at 988 or 1-800-273-8255.

It might not be easy, but it will definitely be worth the effort to do the work to process your difficult experiences and get to the other side. We have put together this workbook and app based on decades of helping people through life's worst moments. We want to help you, too! Good for you for picking up this workbook, or thanks to that caring person who gave it to you. You have taken the first step toward recovery, and you are on your way to the other side of your traumatic experience. Congratulations!

CHAPTER 2

Why Approach Difficult Experiences?

CATCHING UP WITH OUR CASE EXAMPLES

Ann

Think back to Ann, who was raped when she was out at a club. It was the most awful thing that she had ever experienced, and she desperately wanted to pretend like it had never happened. She went out drinking and dancing and using drugs every night for a week after it happened. Ann just wanted to never think about it again, to pretend it had never happened. She had not told anyone about it, and she did not know who had assaulted her. She blamed herself for going to the club alone that night and letting herself be drugged. She was sure that if she told anyone about what happened, they would blame her, too. For the first week afterward, Ann was drinking heavily and using other drugs to numb her feelings of terror and self-blame. After a week of very little sleep and heavy substance use, her body collapsed, and she slept the entire weekend. When she woke up Monday morning, she felt terrified and called in sick to work. From that day forward, until she finally sought treatment, Ann didn't go anywhere except back and forth between work and home, and she never used a restroom with more than one stall in which the main door couldn't be locked.

David

David, the ICU nurse, felt that he had to work as much as he could. The nursing shortage was hitting his hospital hard. He took every extra shift and was constantly working. He rarely took breaks despite his coworkers suggesting that he rest and recharge. His temper was short, and he often complained about people wasting his time. He ate lunch on his own due to pandemic precautions but also because he did not want to bother with people. He felt he was "running on empty," but he had to keep going because the patients and ICU needed him. The memory of Clem's death was returning to him in dreams whenever he tried to sleep. He was not sleeping well. He thought he might as well be working if he could not sleep.

Helen

Returning to Helen after the car accident, once she was out of the hospital and feeling better physically, she made sure to continue going to work and driving the same route she normally drove. At first it was scary and she was nervous to be out on the road again, but after a week she could feel herself starting to relax, and after a month she was almost back to her normal routine. Helen talked to her husband, Andrew, and her friends about the crash and warned people to watch out for semi-trucks that cannot really see cars driving next to them. Her friends and family were supportive and often expressed how worried they had been about her recovery and how happy they were to see her getting back to her life. By talking it out and driving again, even though it was scary, Helen worked through it and didn't have any lasting emotional problems resulting from this car crash.

Miguel

Recall Miguel, who survived an IED explosion in Iraq. With rehabilitation, Miguel was able to walk again, and he tried to pick his life back up where he had left it before he was deployed, but he was having trouble. Miguel went over and over in his head how he "missed" the IED and that he must have been tired and not paying enough attention. He felt that he had failed his unit by not avoiding the IED. He never shared anything about the incident with anyone. His avoidance meant he was not able to get any positive social support from his unit or his family after he returned. In addition, Miguel now felt that, with his injured leg, he was vulnerable to the dangerous world where people are always trying to take advantage of you or hurt you. He felt unable to protect his wife, Lisa, and their girls, and unable to lead his crew at work. The more Miguel felt incompetent, the more hopeless and helpless he became.

Lisa thought it would be good for Miguel to get out of the house and go grocery shopping with her and the girls. When he went out with them, she noticed that he was constantly scanning their surroundings, wouldn't let the girls out of his sight, and would look left and right before they could round the corner to go down a new aisle. Miguel was essentially pulling guard duty, trying to protect his family due to his posttraumatic stress disorder (PTSD). All of these actions are part of hypervigilance in PTSD.

Even though his fellow soldiers came to his support after the IED incident, Miguel believed that they must blame him for the loss of their comrade, and these feelings weigh heavily on him. Rather than face people whom he feels blame him, he withdrew into alcohol and isolation. When Lisa became concerned about his drinking and tried to talk about this with him, Miguel interpreted this as his wife rejecting and criticizing him and what he perceived as his needs.

Miguel withdrew from his family. He was emotionally distant from Lisa and their young daughters, Gabriella and Maria. He was angry, drinking too much, and having problems sleeping. Lisa was trying to help by pointing out how his drinking was impacting the family, but Miguel felt she did not understand his situation and was criticizing him, which further increased his sense of isolation. Lisa finally told him that he had to get treatment. Miguel went to his local VA hospital where he was assessed and diagnosed with PTSD. This "wake-up call" has provided Miguel with the motivation to seek treatment for PTSD.

What is the difference between how Ann, David, Helen, and Miguel reacted to their experiences? Ann tried to pretend the assault didn't happen and drank too much to keep up the pretense. David worked himself to the bone, exhausted and isolated. Miguel also isolated himself and drank alcohol heavily. Only Helen processed the memory of the car crash. And only Helen was able to move on without it haunting her.

These experiences and memories are not easy to think about, but there is no way to the other side of them except through them. As we started to explain in Chapter 1, when very stressful things happen to us, we need to think about them and what they mean to us—what they say about us as a person and how we think about the world. This is called *processing*.

If we don't process these experiences and memories, they can get stuck, intruding into our thoughts over and over and bringing difficult and intense emotions like sadness, fear, or anger. Many people respond to a stressful memory that will not go away by trying to consciously push it away (like Ann), avoiding it and any people, places, or situations that remind them of it. *The problem with avoidance is that the memory keeps coming back and the situation is still there, just unresolved.*

The chapters that follow in *Making Meaning of Difficult Experiences: A Self-Guided Program* (and the Messy Memories app if you choose to use it) will walk you through how to approach stressful memories in a way that will enable you to move through the difficult experience, feel the emotions that you have about the experience in a manageable way, and then move on. Processing the experience and memory in this way will help you think through what happened at the time of the event, how you felt, what you saw, and what that says about you as a person then and now. As you find a place for this stressful memory in your life story and the emotions connected to the memory become less intense, you will be better able to move on with your life without the memory haunting you.

This workbook will help you through many different kinds of unpleasant events, from the stressful to the traumatic. Traumatic events are those in which a person believes they or someone they care about might be killed or seriously injured. Most people recover just fine following stressful or traumatic events, but one reaction that can develop is PTSD. (If you want to learn more, you might want to read our book *PTSD: What Everyone Needs to Know*, which goes into more detail about PTSD and its treatment.)

One of the treatments that has been studied the most for PTSD is called *prolonged exposure* (PE), also known as *exposure therapy*. We have based much of this workbook on what we know helps people following stressful or traumatic experiences, including those who develop PTSD. In exposure therapy, people are helped to confront situations that scare them—but that are realistically safe—in a therapeutic manner to lessen their fear, anxiety, and distress. A classic example of exposure is the advice to a rider to "get back on the horse" after being thrown off. In doing so, the rider overcomes her fear of being thrown again, which prevents the fear from growing. PE helps people approach reminders and memories of the traumatic experience in a safe way, so that their emotional responses of sadness, distress, and other feelings have a chance to decrease and they learn that they can handle them.

This is similar in some ways to the grief process: When we lose someone we love, it is very painful. But by thinking about them and processing the pain, it gradually becomes less painful. Even when situations are not traumatic, this is how we process difficult experiences. Following a stressful event, you need to give yourself the opportunity to learn that you can handle the distress linked to the memory of the event and that your distress will get better if you let yourself revisit the memory—including the emotions you felt at the time. You will find that the distress might increase when you start thinking about the memory but that it doesn't stay high forever. Eventually your stress level will go down, even while you are still thinking about the experience. You will learn that the emotional pain is not unbearable. As you *approach* the memory and reminders instead of *avoiding* them, you can reclaim your life. If your life has become narrow from avoidance (for example, if you have been avoiding people, places, or things that remind you of the difficult experience), you will need to learn to become more active and socially engaged to combat isolation. This workbook will help you.

Approaching and revisiting your memories will help you emotionally process your experiences. *This is a powerful way to learn that the memories of the event(s) are not the same as the event itself.* You will learn that you can safely think about your experience. The anxiety and distress that you may feel at first will recede over time, and you will begin to feel confident that you can tolerate this anxiety and thoughts about this event.

You may believe that thinking about the event makes it feel as if the event is happening all over again, which is partly why you avoid thinking about it. Repeatedly thinking about the event—as we describe in this workbook—will help your brain and your body tell the difference between the past (when the event happened) and the present. This process will help you to realize that although remembering the event can be emotionally upsetting, it is not happening again and therefore *thinking about the event* is not dangerous. Repeated revisiting of the memory may help you think differently about what happened to you. For example, someone who feels guilty about not having done more to resist an attacker may soon realize that she did resist as much as she could have or that the assault might have been even worse if she had resisted more. Similarly, a nurse like David who feels guilty about not being able to save more patients will come to see that the situation was untenable and that COVID-19 was a killer, no matter what he did. You will notice these changes as you revisit the memory over and over, as we suggest.

Right about now, you might be thinking something along the lines of, "But I already obsess about what happened *all the time* as it is—so how is thinking about it *more* going to help?" That's a good question, but in this workbook we are going to do things differently. Let's use an analogy of reading a book. When things are at their worst, you might open this book, get immediately reminded of the event, get triggered, then slam it shut. This may happen many times a day, and you never get close to the end of the book. With our program, however, you will start reading that book from the beginning and read every word over and over again until you finish—and until you can make some sense out of it and read it with less distress. What happened to you is part of your life, and it needs to be incorporated into your story in a way that you can live with and move on to the next chapter of living your life.

AVOIDANCE

Avoidance is what keeps someone from recovering from stressful or traumatic events. Avoidance starts as you retreat to a safe place to recover but then never return to your daily routine because it no longer feels safe. If you begin to feel that you can no longer do the things that matter to you, a sense of failure and incompetence may soon follow. Such feelings feed the avoidance, and your life may become smaller and smaller as you continue to avoid.

You may find that what began as a poorly worded comment from a friend, coworker, police officer, or someone else following the event can take on a life of its own, driving you to isolate yourself and withdraw from life and activities even more.

Ann

Following the rape, Ann heard on the news about a serial rapist who was targeting women at nightclubs. She then heard her coworkers discussing this case at work and saying that any woman who goes to the club alone is putting herself at risk. Her coworkers did not know what had happened to her, but Ann took this as confirmation that if she told anyone what happened they would blame her. In addition, this increased her own self-blame and further convinced her to isolate from people.

It is important to emotionally process a traumatic experience. It is *not* helpful to "soldier on" and avoid thinking about it. As explained earlier, we make analogies to the grief process: the only way to the other side of the pain is through it. Writing or talking about it to others has been shown to reduce many of the negative health effects associated with the trauma and help with readjustment. But not just once: talk about it, talk about it, talk about it, until you don't need to talk about it anymore (or write about it repeatedly, in detail, including your emotional reactions). Unfortunately, no one can say just when things will start to get better. You must talk or write about the experience as much as you need to until you feel better and can get back to living your life. The point is that the troubling memories and debilitating anxiety won't go away on their own. You have to process the experience, and talking or writing about it repeatedly, trying to make sense of it, is one of the best ways to do so. That is what this workbook is for.

EARLY INTERVENTION CAN HELP

We conducted a study of people in the emergency room who had experienced a traumatic event just hours earlier. Our treatment was to have them talk about what had just happened, repeatedly, in the present tense, for about 45 minutes. We recorded that account for them to listen to at home. We also asked them not to avoid safe situations just because these people, places, or experiences reminded them of the traumatic event. We taught them a brief breathing relaxation method to practice and reminded them to take care of themselves and be nice to themselves for the next few days. People who received this treatment had one-half the rate of PTSD 3 months later compared to people who didn't.

Talking about your difficult experience in a therapeutic manner helps—but, as we mentioned, you can also help yourself by not avoiding realistically safe situations just because they remind you of the event. If you were involved in a motor vehicle crash, for example, you need to get back out there and drive right away, making sure to drive the very same vehicle (when and if it is drivable again), along the very same stretch of road where the crash occurred. You need to put yourself in situations that are realistically safe but that may make you uncomfortable—and to stay in them long enough for your body and brain to get used to them and realize that these situations do not pose the level of threat that you might have felt at first. Take a friend along, if you like, but don't become dependent on having someone with you if you used to drive alone. This will enable you to reincorporate those situations into your life so that they become part of your daily routine again rather than a repeated trigger for anxiety relating to the experience.

Helen

Fortunately for Helen, she was brought to the emergency room following her collision where psychologists were conducting a study of an early intervention to try to prevent the development of PTSD, so the study team approached her and asked if she wanted to participate. When her husband, Andrew, heard that this study might prevent the development of PTSD, he encouraged Helen to enroll. After the psychologists described the study, Helen agreed to participate, so the therapist providing the intervention asked some preliminary questions and Helen was officially signed up approximately 3 hours after the crash.

Treatment in the ER

The treatment that Helen received in the ER is the therapy that we describe earlier in this chapter, in which trauma survivors are asked to tell the story of what had just happened, over and over again, in the present tense, while the therapist makes a recording for the survivor to listen to for practice. The therapist had Helen begin her narrative starting before the first impact and describe everything that was happening in the present tense, including everything that she felt, heard, smelled, and thought as though it was happening now.

Helen told her trauma story several times, and she and the therapist discussed the feelings that came up as she told her story. Helen identified effective coping strategies that she had used during the trauma, such as transitioning her fears of dying to thoughts of being "hopeful" and "grateful" while she was riding in the ambulance. She was again scared in the ambulance that she had been seriously injured and feared she would be paralyzed, but she remembered wiggling her toes and fingers and taking that as a good sign. She remembered the EMT's kind words and tone telling her they were just treating her as if she could have spinal injuries, but the EMT thought Helen would be fine. She also incorporated the results of the X-ray that showed no spinal injury and the report of the doctor and nurse that she would be sore for a few days but otherwise would be fine.

What we tell ourselves influences what we feel and do. If we tell ourselves things such as "I can't do this," "It's my fault this happened," or "This is dangerous [when it really isn't]," these negative self-statements can lead us to feel more depressed, guilty, or anxious. On the other hand, positive self-statements such as "I can do this," "I did the best that I could," or "This is OK for me to do" can help us feel better and help motivate us to stay active and not avoid.

Helen was able to generate positive self-statements related to the fact that she survived the situation and believed that good things would come out of the crash, such as being more responsible and caring of others. Additionally, although she felt anger toward the truck driver, she made the decision to focus on the kindness and helpfulness of the bystanders and paramedics, a part of the trauma that became more evident to her as she was retelling her story over and over.

While still in the hospital, the therapist and Helen created a list of things to do for homework over the coming weeks. The policewoman thought that Helen's car would be considered "totaled" by the insurance company, so she was likely going to have to get a new car. In the meantime, the truck driver's insurance would probably pay for a rental car. In response to Helen feeling hesitant to resume her normal driving routine, she and her therapist created a plan in which Helen agreed to first participate in less anxiety-provoking situations such as sitting in the driver's seat with the car turned off and then driving around her neighborhood side streets. They made a plan to get Helen driving herself back to the school where she taught within a week. Helen identified doing yoga and spending time with her family as self-care activities, and she agreed to take the following day as a sick day from work to give herself time to recover and process what happened.

Follow-Up Assessments

One month after the crash, Helen had a follow-up meeting with the therapist, in which Helen reported mild PTSD symptoms. For example, she was overly alert while driving and startled easily. She thought about the crash at least a few times a week and was still nervous when driving, especially in the rain. She continued to talk about what happened with her close family and friends, who were very supportive and noticed that she became more and more comfortable talking about what happened.

At her 3-month follow-up appointment, Helen reported that she did not avoid driving the same highway to work or thinking/talking about the crash and that she knew it would take time for her over-alertness and startle response to go down while driving. She credited the early intervention for helping her because she could imagine having wanted to avoid driving and talking about the crash if the therapist in the ER hadn't encouraged her not to avoid it. She also liked the reframing of some of her scary thoughts that she was going to die or be seriously injured to being grateful that she was alive and focusing on the kindness others showed her.

LIFE AFTER A DIFFICULT EXPERIENCE

Immediately after a very stressful or traumatic event, most people have reactions that could be called PTSD if they were to continue over time; these reactions might include thinking about the event a lot and having strong emotional reactions to things that remind you of it. Over time, however, if you get back to your daily life and back to doing the things that you need and want to do, these reactions tend to lessen. This process is known as *natural recovery*, and it has two important components.

1. You must allow yourself to think about the event and be around people, places, and situations that remind you of the event, and experience the feelings that come up without pushing them away.
2. When you think about what happened and approach/engage with event-related situations, you have the opportunity to learn that *thinking* about the event is not dangerous and also that event-related situations, people, and places are not dangerous either. You will learn that you can do what you need to do in life and that you can handle negative emotions.

By getting back to your life and approaching (rather than avoiding) trauma memories and reminders, you will learn that you can tolerate these situations and that nothing bad happens as a result of the memories alone. You will learn that your feelings of distress will decrease even while you are confronting what you have been avoiding. You will learn that you will not "go crazy" or lose control. Through natural recovery and approaching, you can tell the difference between the traumatic event and other similar but nondangerous events.

WHAT IS POSTTRAUMATIC GROWTH?

Following a traumatic event, most people eventually recover and do not suffer with mental health issues in the long term. In addition, some people report positive changes following stressful or traumatic events. This *posttraumatic growth* refers to a sense of positive change following exposure to traumatic experiences. *Resilience* is by far the more common outcome for survivors. We continue to be surprised at the strength and fortitude of the human spirit to make it out of tough circumstances and go on to survive and thrive. Many people experience a sense of accomplishment for making it out of a tough situation or for surviving the trauma. Others realize that before the event they did not know what was important to them, whereas, after surviving, they have a real sense of how precious life can be and they feel that their values are more in line with their lives as a result. Some people learn that they can trust their instincts, which can feel very reassuring. Some who are religious say that God saved them for a reason, and now they need to find that reason. Others witnessed acts of pure heroism or selflessness and now know that people are capable of such behavior.

CAN'T WE JUST ERASE THE MEMORY?

You may have wondered whether you could just erase the trauma memory from your brain entirely. We understand: it is common for people to wish it had never happened, and, since we can't change the past, it's natural to think that the next best thing might be to erase the memory so that you can act like it never happened.

Ann

Ann did all that she could to try and forget the rape had happened, but despite all the drugs and drinking and trying to stay busy, she knew it had happened. The memory haunted her, and she continued to have nightmares every time she closed her eyes. Eventually she realized that she needed help to move past the rape.

When she spoke to a therapist for the first time, Ann asked if there was any way to just take the memory out of her head.

While that is not possible, revisiting the memory (as this workbook will teach you to do) should reduce the intensity of the emotions connected to it so that you can think through what it means about you and the world in a new way. Often this process can result in your noticing things that you did to survive or to help others and to feel good about these behaviors. Seeing and acknowledging your own competence during a stressful time can go a long way toward helping you feel capable of handling the memory and interacting with the world again. In addition, once the intensity of your emotion is less, you might find that you can reconsider some of the assumptions or conclusions you made that are unhelpful or wrong.

For Ann, after repeatedly recounting the memory of that night in the club when she was assaulted and processing the experience, this involved reconsidering her conclusions that (1) she was stupid for going to the club on her own that evening, and (2) she was just asking for someone to take advantage of her. She was able to see that the rapist did not target her specifically but instead was waiting to victimize anyone's drink he could spike and then follow them into the restroom stall. He was a sexual predator, and this was premeditated. She was able to recognize that it was OK for a woman to go to a club alone. She would not blame her friend if she had gone to a club alone and was assaulted. Ann was in the wrong place at the wrong time, but not because she did anything wrong. She did not need to be ashamed of herself or blame herself. In fact, just the opposite: Ann needed to have compassion for herself.

WHAT ABOUT WHEN PEOPLE DON'T WANT TO FORGET?

You may feel that changing how you think about what happened would dishonor the memory of others who endured it with you or who didn't survive. We often hear this from veterans who talk about fellow servicemembers who died, or even about fellow survivors. For instance, Miguel felt guilty that he survived and his friend, Russo, did not. He felt that if he was less upset about the IED incident this somehow meant he was forgetting about Russo's sacrifice. We have also heard this from healthcare workers who witnessed so many deaths due to COVID-19. For these survivors, like David discussed earlier in this chapter, there is often an aspect of the memory that is positive and affirming of their work and the work of others. They fear that if they process the pain of the trauma they might forget people they care about—their brothers and sisters in arms, or patients, or fellow healthcare workers. If you feel like this, it is important to remember that revisiting the memory does not remove it; it simply reduces the intensity of the associated *negative* emotion and distress. You couldn't forget your comrades, or patients, or people you lost even if you tried—and we are not suggesting you do. Instead, we hope that by working on these memories so that they cause you less distress, you can have a greater sense of remembrance and begin to see the *positives* within the tough event that you endured. If the situation were reversed and you had not survived, would you want your friends and loved ones to live a good life, one not haunted by what happened? We think so. Life is precious, and those close to you surely would want you to live it fully.

WHAT ABOUT PEOPLE WHO FEEL THE MEMORY IS TAKING OVER THEIR LIVES?

You may feel that the traumatic event has shaped who you are now. You may not necessarily want to lose that sense of yourself, but you also don't want the memory to keep taking over whenever you think about it. The processing of traumatic or stressful memories will allow you to move through the memory in a new way. Once the distress associated with the memory is reduced, you will have the chance to go back and consider all that happened at the time, what you did and did not do, what factors may have contributed to making the decisions you made at the time, what context led to this thing happening, and so on. Through this processing of the memory, you can figure out what you want to take and learn from the event and the memory, as well as what you might change about how you think about the event (what you might want to let go). You will develop a fuller and more complete sense of the event, its context, and what it says about you as a person—both then and now. You will incorporate the event into the narrative of your life and who you are as a person without being defined by it.

WHAT IS GOOD ADVICE FOLLOWING A TRAUMATIC OR STRESSFUL EVENT?

We hear advice for how to take care of ourselves every time we fly: if the oxygen mask drops, place your mask on your face first before assisting others. People very often try to help others first, placing their own needs last. Especially following a traumatic event, when others' needs are so great, some of us may not be able to stop trying to help. We see this often following mass or natural disasters and certainly during the COVID-19 pandemic: responders and providers such as David see such great need that they work double and triple and even quadruple shifts and then fall over exhausted. If we deplete ourselves, we are of no use to others. *It is always important and allowable to take care of yourself.* You are not being selfish: you are being smart and responsible.

In Chapter 1, we discussed some common difficult experiences that may be hard to process, and in this chapter we present why it is so important to not avoid these memories and process them instead. In Chapter 3, we'll coach you through how to do just that. Remember, if processing weren't difficult, you wouldn't need it! Keep going—you'll be glad you did.

How to Approach Difficult Experiences: Memory Exposure and Processing

CATCHING UP WITH OUR CASE EXAMPLES

Ann

After doing all that she could to try to push the rape memory away, Ann finally decided that she needed to ask for help. Avoidance was not working. The memory remained and even felt like it was more in control of her life than ever. Ann decided that the drinking, using, and running around were not working. She did not want to continue to feel bad every morning, and she stopped drinking alcohol and using drugs. As she started to talk with her friends again without substance use, she was able to feel more connected. After meeting once with a therapist, she did not want to go through therapy and instead used the Making Meaning of Difficult Experiences program to approach and process the memory of the rape so that she could take her life back.

David

David realized that he had to do something different when he nearly passed out while assisting with a gunshot wound victim. David had not been eating right and had skipped his break for the second time that day. He felt light-headed and had to ask someone else to step in for him. David suddenly realized that he was not taking care of himself, and this was impacting his care of patients. A detailed account of his work using the worksheets of the Making Meaning of Difficult Experiences program is included at the end of this chapter.

Miguel

In the case of Miguel this was clear: he was proud of his military service and friends, and he felt a sense of accomplishment for the many combat missions he had completed. At the same time, he felt he was to blame for the IED incident in which his friend died. Indeed, for Miguel, his family and his sense of accomplishment are what drove him to go to the VA for treatment when urged by his wife, Lisa. He thought the VA providers might be able to understand his situation.

Shaquila

In the case of Shaquila, she was haunted by the loss of her pregnancy. She had learned from the doctor that they thought she should be able to carry a baby and the loss was not due to any issues with her body but just because many pregnancies never make it to term. Even with this news she was really having a hard time moving past the loss. She spoke with Tanja about her difficulties and Tanja was so happy to see Shaquila reaching out for help after months of isolation. They found this book online and decided to give it a shot.

It is not easy to manage memories from difficult experiences. As we saw in Chapter 2, there is no way to the other side of these memories except by going through them. In this chapter, we explain *how* to approach these memories so that you can begin to move through them and come out the other side with resilience and the ability to thrive. The stories of David, Miguel, Ann, and Shaquila show how avoidance can stall recovery after a difficult experience. Avoidance can also leave us stuck in the difficult experience without a way to move forward. When a difficult experience happens, think about what it means to you as a person, what it says about you, and how you think about the world. Sometimes we come to realize that our first thoughts aren't accurate or helpful (for example, "It was my fault"), and we then need to reevaluate how we think about things. *This is what we mean by processing.*

If you don't process these memories, they get stuck in your head. You end up thinking about them over and over, which leads to difficult and intense emotions like sadness, fear, guilt, or anger. Many people respond to memories of difficult experiences by trying to consciously push them away and avoid the people, places, or situations that remind them of the event. The problem with avoidance, as we have explained several times already, is that the memory keeps coming back as unfinished business.

SO LET'S GET STARTED

Making Meaning of Difficult Experiences: A Self-Guided Program will teach you how to approach stressful memories in a way that enables you to move through them, feel the emotions you have about the experience in a manageable way, and then get back to your life. This is what we call *processing the difficult memory*, and it will help you think through

- what happened at the time of the stressful event,
- what you experienced,
- how you felt,
- what you saw,
- what you and others did or didn't do, and
- what all of this says about you as a person then and now.

For all activities in this workbook, you can choose to complete the printed worksheets in the chapters, or you may choose to audio-record the memory using the Messy Memories app available from the Apple App Store or Google Play. (The printed worksheets appear all together near the end of this workbook in Appendix A, and can be accessed by searching for this book's title on the Oxford Academic platform, at academic.oup.com.) As you find a place for this stressful memory in your life story, and as the emotions connected to the difficult experience become less intense, you will be better able to move on with your life and do what you want to do without having the memory haunt you.

Let's check in now with how you are feeling, and we will keep checking in as you work on the activities throughout this workbook. Part of what you will learn is how to check in with yourself and, if necessary, how to change the work you are doing so that it is most effective for you.

> Always remember, if you feel like speaking with a professional or if you need more help than this workbook can provide, you can use the resources found in Appendix C, "Additional Resources." If you are in crisis, call the National Suicide Prevention Lifeline at 988. There is always someone there to talk to any time of the day or night.

CHECKING IN WITH YOURSELF

Most of us recognize when we are hungry and that we need to eat something; when we feel tired, we understand that is a sign to go to sleep. However, sometimes recognizing what's going on with our emotions and what that means can be more difficult. Taking stock of how you feel can be a great way to boost resilience and learn what works for you and what you need to change. What you do and what you think affect how you feel and function. Assessing yourself in this way can also take the mystery out of how you're feeling. For example, maybe you're not just "having a bad day," and using some of the skills from this workbook may help you feel better. You will learn the connection between feeling and doing. Just like feeling hungry is a cue to eat, paying attention to how you're feeling can be a cue to take care of yourself.

Decide if you want to do these check-ins here in the *Making Meaning of Difficult Experiences* workbook or using the Messy Memories app. If you choose to record your work here in the book, fill out a copy of Worksheet 3.1: Mood Thermometers, showing how you have been doing over the past week for each emotion. We provide one copy of this worksheet near the end of this chapter and additional copies in Appendix A, so you can use those as you move through the book and continue to check in with yourself. If you would like to see how ICU nurse David completed his memory exposure and processing worksheets, take a look at the example at the end of this chapter (pages 48–60).

Now look at what *you* marked on Worksheet 3.1. Since you are just beginning the *Making Meaning of Difficult Experiences* program, this is your starting point, also referred to as your *baseline score*. You will be able to compare how you are feeling at different times to this starting point. We suggest you complete a copy of Worksheet 3.1 about once per week when you are working on a difficult experience. Please feel free to make more copies and make notes on these worksheets.

Think about the specific things going on in your life, including the difficult experience and messy memories that may be contributing to your emotions. Keep in mind that *emotions are not bad*. Rather, emotions tell us how we are relating to the world. They give us information, just like feeling hungry gives us information that it's time to eat. When things are going well for you, positive emotions tell you that you should continue doing what you are doing or maybe even think about doing more and being grateful. However, when difficult experiences occur or when you hit bumps in your life, your negative emotions tell you that something is not working for you; these negative emotions may even suggest what needs to change or they may be letting you know that you are working through something difficult. You can ride the wave of this negative emotion (this feeling won't last forever) and learn from it.

For example, think about the last time you felt angry. What was going on that made you feel angry? Anger often comes when we feel that people are not taking our needs into account or maybe that they are intentionally harming us in some way. Feeling angry can be helpful when you notice the emotion and then consider if there is some way to address the cause of the anger.

Ann

Think back to the story of Ann, who survived a sexual assault when she was out at a club. Her friend Samantha noticed that Ann was drinking a lot and spending a lot of time alone, so

Samantha approached Ann and asked about what was going on and if she needed any help. Ann got really angry and yelled at Samantha, who left abruptly. Afterward, Ann was sad and realized that she had felt so angry because she was defensive, feeling it was her fault she had been assaulted since she had gone to the club alone. Ann also hates asking for help. She did not want to talk to anyone about the rape, and she knew that she was drinking and using drugs way too much. Ann realized she overreacted, so, a few days later, she called Samantha to apologize for her outburst, and the two friends met for dinner that evening. During the meal, Ann was able to tell Samantha what happened at the club and that she needed help and had not been ready to ask for it earlier. Samantha had hit on a nerve, and Ann's anger was a signal of that pain. Samantha was understanding, assured Ann it was not her fault, and offered to do anything she could to help. Samantha had heard about this workbook; she bought a copy for Ann and encouraged her to work through her awful experience.

EMOTIONS ARE NOT DANGEROUS

Emotions are not dangerous or good or bad. Obviously, some emotions don't feel good, and others feel very good. Emotions are signals that we can pay attention to and consider if and how we should respond. Emotions provide us with information about ourselves and our situations. When we have strong reactions, that often means we need to step back and look at the situation to see what may need to happen.

Humans are hard-wired for emotions. When emotions are triggered, what happens next can feel automatic, like the emotion has set off a pattern of behavior. For example,

- When we are scared, there is often a pattern for one of the "three F's"—fight, flee, or freeze.
- When we feel love, there is often a pattern for physical closeness and caretaking.
- When we feel angry, there are likely to be defensive patterns such as Ann exhibited when Samantha struck a nerve.

Looking back at your ratings on Worksheet 3.1: Mood Thermometers, what do you notice? Are there any specific emotions that you rated very high or low that you want to change? What in your life right now may be influencing those emotions to be high or low? To help you figure this out, track your emotions on thermometers about once per week while you are working through *Making Meaning of Difficult Experiences*. Use the Mood Thermometers worksheets located in Appendix A or on the Messy Memories app. (Remember, worksheets also can be accessed by searching for this book's title on the Oxford Academic platform, at academic.oup.com.)

Watch for how your ratings change over time. Are they changing in the direction you want? Are they getting worse?

> *While you are processing a difficult experience, really feeling the emotions that come up is critical.* You may feel that things are getting worse before they get better; your ratings may go up before they go down, and that is OK. It's a sign that you are getting in touch with your emotions, which is good. Increasing emotions does *not* mean that our program will not work for you. Stick with it and feel the emotions to get to the other side. You have seen that avoiding your emotions or the memories or reminders doesn't work. You're here to try something different.

LEARNING TO PROCESS A DIFFICULT EXPERIENCE

Now that you have completed your first copy of Worksheet 3.1: Mood Thermometers and have an idea of where you are starting, the first step for processing a difficult experience is deciding which specific experience or messy memory you want to approach instead of avoid. One way to figure out which memory to work on first is to look at which specific memory is connected to intrusive thoughts and avoidance. (For example, what memory comes back to you in dreams or when you sit down to watch TV?) You might also start with the memory that is related to people, places, or situations that you avoid. (For instance, if you know you will not go to a restaurant alone because you met the man who raped you at a restaurant, the rape may be the memory to work on.) If there is more than one such experience or memory, we suggest you pick the one that is the most upsetting to you right now, the one that is bothering you the most or feeling the most intense, or the one that you are avoiding the most this week.

Once you have selected the memory to work on, decide *when* this memory begins and ends—that is, when did you first feel like the situation became difficult or scary, until the moment when you felt that the particular situation was over. If this is an ongoing or long event, such as caring for COVID-19 patients during the pandemic, try to pick one event that was the worst, the first, or representative and that you reexperience or avoid. For example, combat veterans will often pick the first event in which they felt that someone could die or in which someone did die. They will often tell us, "It wasn't the worst thing I experienced over there, but it is the one that sticks with me."

Miguel

For Miguel, who had significant combat experience during his deployment, the IED attack stuck with him due to the loss of Russo. That made it more painful for Miguel. They had come through so many combat missions without injury or incident and to lose his friend so suddenly and then be pulled away from his unit made it even worse.

If something is haunting you, that is the one to work on.

If you're having difficulty picking a specific memory, just focus on one event, or one slice of time to get started. You can always work on another memory once you finish the first one. *Memory processing works best if you stick with one memory at a time and work on it until it no longer feels stuck or so overwhelming.*

Using Worksheet 3.2: Difficult Experience Writing Exercise, located at the end of this chapter and in Appendix A near the end of this workbook, write down your difficult experience memory or use the Messy Memories app to record it on your phone. If you choose to use the app, the worksheets are built in. Remember, David's completed worksheets are shown on pages 48–60.

Keep your *Making Meaning of Difficult Experiences* workbook in a safe and private place. When doing memory processing, it is important to include all details of the memory—especially the most upsetting details—and we don't want you to worry that someone else could read what you write. Let yourself feel the emotions that come up. DO NOT AVOID. There may come a time when it will be good for you to talk about what happened with someone, but this memory exposure and processing part is just for you. If you think it will be more secure to record the memory on your phone in the Messy Memories app, we encourage you to do so.

As noted on Worksheet 3.2: Difficult Experience Writing Exercise, describe the difficult experience memory in the present tense, as if it is happening now. "I am in the ICU" or "I am driving my car on the interstate" are examples of this kind of present-focused writing. Please include all the details you can remember about what *you* are seeing, hearing, smelling, and doing; what *others* are doing and saying; and what other people look like. If it is in your memory, write it down, or say it out loud if you are using the Messy Memories app. No one else needs to see this but you, so write it all down. Let yourself feel the emotions. Be present with the memory, feeling what you felt at the time. Let the emotions come up and go away as you move through the memory.

Tips for Recounting Memories

When recounting the memories, it is important to include details, such as

1. The stimuli (people, places, and things) that bring up emotional reactions,
2. Your responses (e.g., my heart is racing), and
3. The meaning you associate with the stimuli (e.g., he's going to die) and the meaning you associate with your responses (e.g., fast heartbeat means you are terrified).

Don't worry if you feel like you can't remember everything; that's normal—just write what you can remember. Don't worry about how it sounds, or the words you use, or the grammar or punctuation. Don't write it thinking how it would sound to someone else. This is for you to see. This skill works best if you stay with one difficult experience until it no longer feels stuck or so overwhelming.

You'll want to choose the right time to work on this difficult experience exercise—a time when you can devote your full attention to it, when you have privacy, and not right before bedtime. Especially the first time you complete this activity, allow yourself a few minutes to process following the experience.

Every time you practice this skill, we recommend that you go through the story of your difficult experience memory three times: once each week you will write it out once and then read it over at least twice or for 20 to 30 minutes (whichever is longer), adding more detail or focus as you go. Please spend at least 20 to 30 minutes each time you work on a difficult memory "exposure." For the review sessions, you will read through the memory at least three times or for 20 to 30 minutes. Make sure to let yourself *feel your emotions* throughout the exercise. Do not try to control your emotions or keep them in check, and do not stop in the middle of the writing or reading or recording. After each recounting session, think about and then answer a few questions about the difficult experience; these will help you to revisit the messy memory again and possibly see it in a different light or consider what you need or want to work on.

Refer to David's memory exposure and processing worksheets (on pages 48–60) to help you see how everything fits together.

Tips for Processing a Difficult Memory

1. Make sure you have privacy and at least 20 to 30 minutes to devote your full attention to the exercise. Do not do this right before bed.

2. Pick the memory that has been bothering you the most over the past week.

3. Decide when this difficult experience begins (when things start to get difficult) and ends (when you feel relatively safe again).

4. Write out the selected memory once per week using Worksheet 3.2: Difficult Experience Writing Exercise or the Messy Memories app. After you write it once, read it over at least twice or for 20 to 30 minutes, whichever is longer.

5. Write about the difficult experience in the present tense, as though it is happening now.

6. Include all the details you can remember. This includes all your thoughts, feelings, things you did, sensory details (such as what you smell, hear, see, or feel on your skin), and anything that helps you feel present with the memory.

7. *Most importantly*, let yourself *feel your emotions* throughout the exercise. Include your emotions in what you are writing; for example, "I am terrified when I see the truck heading for me and realize it is going to hit me."

8. Do not stop in the middle of the writing, reading, or recording.

9. Process the difficult experience memory (what you wrote about on Worksheet 3.2) using Worksheet 3.3: Difficult Experience Processing Exercise, located near the end of this chapter and in Appendix A, choosing the questions that feel most useful for you and your memory on that day.

10. Choose one of the Worksheets 3.5 to 3.8: Exploring Emotions in Your Difficult Experience, to review on that day.

11. Review Worksheet 3.2: Difficult Experience Writing Exercise at least three times per week or even daily if you would like. For each review, read the memory at least three times or for at least 20 to 30 minutes and complete a record of your review using Worksheet 3.4: Daily Review of the Difficult Experience Writing Exercise, which can be found near the end of this chapter and in Appendix A.

12. After each daily review, process the difficult experience memory using Worksheet 3.3: Difficult Experience Processing Exercise, choosing the questions that feel most useful for you and your memory on that day. You can review these questions and think about them daily, and complete this form weekly. Again, feel free to write notes on the worksheets—they are for you.

13. After each daily review, choose one of the Worksheets 3.5 to 3.8: Exploring Emotions in Your Difficult Experience (all of which can be found near the end of this chapter and also in Appendix A) to review on that day. The selected worksheet may be the same one you completed previously or a new one. Think about what may be most useful for you on that day. Please complete a worksheet weekly, but think about these emotions as you review and think about this memory.

14. Continue working with one difficult experience memory until it no longer feels stuck or overwhelming to you. You may notice this in lower distress scores or in just feeling less intense emotions when you approach the memory exercises.

15. Use this workbook in a way that works for you. You can read and practice a chapter per week, adding to your skills and healthy habits practice, or start working on them all sooner. We have included enough worksheets for 6 weeks, but feel free to make copies or use the app or download copies from the website.

LET'S BEGIN

Just before you begin your own exposure and processing exercise, make sure you have privacy and no distractions. Allow yourself plenty of time so you are not worried about how long this takes, especially this first time. Try to minimize noise and other distractions, which could interrupt your memory processing. We suggest you silence your phone. We walk you through the worksheet here but if you prefer to use the app it will walk you through memory exposure and processing.

Using Worksheet 3.2: Difficult Experience Writing Exercise (on page 40), begin by showing how *Distressed* you are feeling about revisiting the experience *right now* by marking your level of distress along the thermometer at the start of the worksheet. (Remember, worksheets appear at the end of the chapters and also in Appendix A at the end of this workbook.)

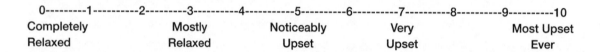

```
0---------1----------2---------3----------4-----------5----------6----------7----------8----------9----------10
Completely              Mostly               Noticeably           Very                    Most Upset
Relaxed                 Relaxed              Upset                Upset                   Ever
```

After you have rated your distress, begin to write down the memory of your difficult experience, following the directions on Worksheet 3.2. What you write does not have to be pretty. When you finish writing out your memory once, review it twice or for 20 to 30 minutes, whichever is longer. Then record how you feel on the distress thermometer as well the highest level of distress you felt while approaching the memory today.

We suggest that you write out a new version of the difficult experience once per week. You can see how the memory changes over time as you work on it. We also suggest that you read/review the most current version of the memory each day. For each review, read the memory at least three times or for at least 20 to 30 minutes and complete a record of your review using Worksheet 3.4: Daily Review of the Difficult Experience Writing Exercise. Some people find that they remember more details as they are reading through this exercise; if this is true for you, it is fine to add additional details as you are rereading your difficult experience.

BEGINNING TO PROCESS THE MEMORY

After you finish doing the difficult experience exercise, think about how it went. Keep in mind that everyone processes difficult experiences differently. There is no one pattern of distress that is needed to move through a memory to the other side. In the many years we have worked with trauma survivors, we have seen thousands of different patterns of distress. What is most important is to approach the difficult experience memory, stay with it, and feel the emotions it brings up without pushing them away. Go back and approach it again and again until the memory is no longer distressing or until you feel like you can handle the distress the memory brings up. Try to be realistic in your expectations of yourself. For example, if your difficult experience involved someone's death, that will always be sad, but maybe it doesn't have to feel so intensely distressing. Many difficult experiences will never feel neutral and are things that never should have happened or that you wish hadn't happened, but you won't have to feel stuck or avoid the memories.

In our many years of experience working with survivors of trauma, we have seen several common memory processing patterns. For some people the distress associated with the memory starts out at a high level and reduces the first time they approach it. These people may quickly see that going through the memory of the event and sticking with the feelings can result in feeling less upset when thinking about this memory.

For some people, the distress may stay high throughout the exercise or even increase as they let themselves feel the emotions and approach the memory more closely. The good news is that if they stick with the processing exercise over time and continue approaching the memory despite difficulty, the distress typically goes down the more they approach the memory, and they can take their life back from the difficult experience.

While processing a difficult memory, people often remember important details that change how they think about their difficult experience. These remembered details may increase distress or decrease distress. For example, some people feel haunted by a difficult experience because they think they did not do enough, but, when revisiting the memory as we suggest here, they see that they actually did everything they could. Remembering additional details is normal and part of the process for some people but not required, and we have never seen people remember details that they couldn't handle.

Keep in mind that staying with the process to ride the wave through the memory is how you get to the other side. It is common when we do this work with people in person that they say they can't do it when we get to the hardest part of the memory, but by sticking with it even when it is difficult, they learn that they can get through it and that is how it gets better. Hold yourself accountable. If it wasn't difficult, you wouldn't need this program. Sticking with the memory work and processing is how to make it easier. If at any time it feels like too much, reach out to your social connections discussed in Chapter 5, or review Appendix C for additional resources.

It is common for some people to rush through the memory their first time approaching it and then include much more detail and emotion as they go through it again. We encourage you to try not to rush through and to include as many details and emotions as you can. As with most things in life, you get out of it what you put into it.

When some people approach a difficult experience memory, they get stuck trying to fix it or focus on why it happened to them, or they spin their wheels rather than focusing on *feeling* the emotions that they felt at the time of the event. This is called *rumination,* and it can sometimes intensify these negative emotions. If you are finding yourself spinning your wheels while trying to approach the memory, you may be ruminating. Next time you do the memory exercise, try focusing on the emotions you felt at the time of the difficult experience without trying to fix what happened or change your feelings or wonder why this happened to you. Just describe what happened as it unfolded and be there with the emotion; see how this may feel different and change how the exercise feels for you. If you try this and still continue to get stuck in rumination after a few attempts, this exercise may not be the way you need to work on the difficult experience, and you may need more direction from a mental health professional trained in exposure therapy. We have included resources in Appendix C. We suggest you try to either switch to another memory and see if it works differently when you approach it or skip to another skill (for example, increasing your social connections [Chapter 5] or engaging in self-care [Chapter 6]) to see if some of the other skills are a better fit for you.

PROCESSING THE MEANING OF THE DIFFICULT EXPERIENCE

As we note above, after you reach the end of your difficult experience memory exercise, take time to think about how it went and what the memory says about you as a person then and now. This is the heart of processing.

The First Step

If this is the first time you worked on this difficult experience, think about how it went compared to how you expected it to go. Was it easier or harder than you thought it would be? Why? Did the emotions come easily and intensely, or was it difficult to connect with the emotion? If this is not your first time through the difficult experience, compare it to previous times. Is it getting easier? Are you remembering new information or thinking about it in a different way?

Celebrate your success in approaching the memory and celebrate any signs that it may be getting easier to approach. If it doesn't get easier as fast as you would like, celebrate the fact that you are doing the hard work and you are tolerating the distress. Exposure isn't meant to work after just one time, so you may need to remind yourself to be patient.

The Second Step

The next step of processing a difficult experience is diving into the meaning of the memory. Worksheet 3.3: Difficult Experience Processing Exercise is designed to help you think through the meaning of the memory and how that meaning may be changing over time and as you are approaching the difficult experience memory. The list of questions in the worksheet covers the most common questions we have used when working with trauma survivors over our combined 50-plus years of practice. That said, we do not expect all the questions to be important for all people who are working on difficult experiences. We recommend trying to answer all the questions the first time you do the exercise and then pick and choose those you think are more productive for you. Keep in mind that this may change over time as you approach the memory. We suggest you complete this worksheet once weekly.

The Third Step

The last step in processing the difficult experiences memory is exploring emotions connected to the difficult experience. This part of processing focuses on the emotions you felt during the difficult experience itself as well as the emotions you felt during the memory exposure exercise. Depending on the main emotion you felt as you were approaching the difficult experience memory, select one of the Exploring Emotions in Your Difficult Experience worksheets (3.5 to 3.8) to help walk you through this step in the process. The worksheets can be found near the end of this chapter as well as in Appendix A near the end of this workbook. We suggest you complete one of these worksheets at least once weekly.

The emotions you experience may be different from what others feel and often include both positive (lucky, grateful, etc.) and negative emotions (sad, anxious, scared, guilty, angry, etc.). Each time you are working on a difficult experience choose one exploring emotion to focus on. Once you have completed one Exploring Emotions in Your Difficult Experience worksheet, you can decide if you have worked on this skill enough for one day or whether you want to look at another emotion. You will see that the worksheets focus on the negative emotions and not the happy ones. This is because the negative emotions are what keep people stuck in the difficult experience. We naturally want to avoid things that make us feel scared, guilty, ashamed, angry, and so on. Examining your emotions and thoughts can help change how you think and feel about this difficult experience, and that's the goal of this program!

Does the emotion you feel when approaching the difficult experience make sense given the experience and how long it has been since the difficult event occurred? For instance, if the difficult experience is the loss of a loved one that occurred last week, it is normal to continue to be intensely sad for weeks and maybe even longer. If you think the emotion makes sense, giving yourself room and time to feel it can be helpful to allow you to naturally move through the experience to the other side. Consider how to give yourself that space and ways to care for yourself while you are feeling the emotions over time.

If, however, you think the emotion is more intense than it needs to be or is hanging around longer than is needed, think about whether you are ready to let the emotion go and what you want or need to do to release that emotion. Going back to the example of grieving, if the loss was months or years ago, sometimes letting go can just involve remembering the good times with the person and acknowledging they are gone. For others, it may require an outward sign of the change, like visiting the grave or creating a scrapbook. If you think you would feel guilty about having less pain about the loss, work on that. Consider what might work for you to let go of the emotion when you are ready. Worksheets 3.5 to 3.8 guide you through common emotions that can keep people stuck. You can walk through how David used the difficult experience memory processing on pages 48–60 to see how it worked for him.

WHEN ARE YOU DONE WITH MEMORY EXPOSURE OF THE DIFFICULT EXPERIENCE?

We suggest that you continue to work on the difficult experience memory until it no longer feels stuck. If you start feeling bored—rather than distressed—you will know it is time to work on another memory or move to another skill. People often find that after approaching a difficult experience with memory exposure, they feel generally more confident and able to handle memories of the difficult experiences as they come up. At the very least, you will have a new skill for approaching difficult experience memories when they happen that will allow you to feel the emotion raised by the memory, stay with it, share it, and let it go. If life gets difficult, you will have the skills to get through it.

WORKSHEET 3.1: Mood Thermometers

Date: _____

Make a mark on each line that describes how you have been feeling on *average* over the *past week*. We suggest you complete a new version of this worksheet once per week while working on the program.

0---------1---------2---------3---------4---------5---------6---------7---------8---------9--------10
Calm   Neutral   Anxious

0---------1---------2---------3---------4---------5---------6---------7---------8---------9--------10
Happy   Neutral   Sad

0---------1---------2---------3---------4---------5---------6---------7---------8---------9--------10
Peaceful   Neutral   Angry

0---------1---------2---------3---------4---------5---------6---------7---------8---------9--------10
Organized   Neutral   Disorganized

0---------1---------2---------3---------4---------5---------6---------7---------8---------9--------10
Socially Connected   Neutral   Isolated

0---------1---------2---------3---------4---------5---------6---------7---------8---------9--------10
Proud   Neutral   Ashamed

WORKSHEET 3.2: Difficult Experience Writing Exercise

Date: _____

Rate your distress right BEFORE completing the difficult experience exercise:

0---------1---------2----------3----------4---------5----------6---------7----------8----------9---------10
Completely Relaxed   Noticeably Upset   Most Distressed Ever

Describe your difficult experience below. Begin from the moment in the memory when you feel it getting difficult or messy and end at the moment when you feel the immediate risk or event is over. Include all the details that let you connect with the memory, including what you see, what you feel in your body, what you think, and how the details unfold. Let yourself feel the emotions as they come up. Do not avoid or push them away. Revisit the memory by writing in the present tense as though it is happening now. When you finish writing it out once, review it twice or for 20 to 30 minutes, whichever is longer. Please feel free to use additional pages.

_____

_____

_____

_____

_____

_____

_____

_____

_____

_____

_____

_____

_____

_____

_____

_____

_____

_____

_____

_____

_____

_____

_____

_____

_____

_____

_____

_____

_____

_____

_____

How long did you work on the difficult experience exercise? _____ minutes

Rate your distress right AFTER completing the difficult experience exercise:

0---------1---------2----------3----------4---------5----------6---------7----------8----------9---------10
Completely Relaxed   Noticeably Upset   Most Distressed Ever

Rate the HIGHEST level of your distress during the difficult experience exercise:

0---------1---------2----------3----------4---------5----------6---------7----------8----------9---------10
Completely Relaxed   Noticeably Upset   Most Distressed Ever

Review Worksheet 3.2: Difficult Experience Writing Exercise, at least three times per week or even daily if you would like. For each review, read the memory at least three times or for at least 20 to 30 minutes and complete a record of your review using Worksheet 3.4: Daily Review of the Difficult Experiences Writing Exercise.

WORKSHEET 3.3: Difficult Experience Processing Exercise

Please complete this worksheet once weekly and review the processing questions after each 20- to 30-minute difficult experience writing exercise (Worksheet 3.2) or after a difficult experience daily review (Worksheet 3.4). If you need more space for any question, just grab a sheet of paper and keep writing.

1. Why did this happen to you? What was the cause? _____

_____

_____

2. How did the difficult experience change how you think about yourself? _____

_____

_____

3. How did the difficult experience change how you think about others? _____

_____

_____

4. How did the difficult experience change how you see the world? _____

_____

_____

5. After completing Worksheets 3.2 or 3.4, what new, different, or important information did you notice today? _____

_____

6. What would you tell your family member, loved one, or friend if this had happened to them?

_____

_____

WORKSHEET 3.4: Daily Review of the Difficult Experience Writing Exercise

Review Worksheet 3.2: Difficult Experience Writing Exercise at least three times per week or even daily if you would like. For each review, read the memory at least three times or for at least 20 to 30 minutes and complete a record of your review using this Worksheet to record your distress just prior to, during, and just after each difficult experience daily review. Remember, we suggest that each difficult experience daily review includes

1. Reading the difficult memory from the Difficult Experience Writing Exercise (Worksheet 3.2) at least three times or 20 minutes—whichever is longer.
2. Completing a Difficult Experience Processing Exercise (Worksheet 3.3) once per week or reviewing this week's version.
3. Completing your choice of the Exploring Emotions in Your Difficult Experience (Worksheets 3.5 to 3.8) once per week or reviewing this week's version.

Use the following scale to rate your distress:

0---------1---------2---------3---------4---------5---------6---------7---------8---------9---------10
Completely   Mostly   Noticeably   Very   Most Upset
Relaxed   Relaxed   Upset   Upset   Ever

Date of review	Minutes reviewed	Distress level right BEFORE reviewing the difficult experience (0–10)	Distress level right AFTER reviewing the difficult experience (0–10)	HIGHEST level of distress reviewing the difficult experience (0–10)

WORKSHEET 3.5: Exploring Emotions in Your Difficult Experience:

SADNESS

Please choose which Exploring Emotions in Your Difficult Experience worksheet/s (Worksheets 3.5 to 3.8) you want to review after each 20- to 30-minute difficult experience writing exercise (Worksheet 3.2) OR difficult experience daily review (Worksheet 3.4). Complete this worksheet once weekly and review it with each daily review. If you need more space for any question, just grab a sheet of paper and keep writing.

1. Do you feel like this sadness is similar to how most people would be feeling at this point since the event?   YES   NO   I AM NOT SURE

If you answered YES, letting yourself grieve this loss or situation makes sense. Letting yourself feel sadness can often be the best way to move through sadness to the other side. What can you do to care for yourself while you grieve? _____

_____

If you answered NO or I AM NOT SURE, why do you think this level of sadness is sticking with you?

_____

_____

2. Are you ready to let the sadness go?   YES   NO   I AM NOT SURE

If you answered NO or I AM NOT SURE, what do you need to be ready to let the sadness go? HINT: Only YOU can decide when to let the sadness go. _____

_____

If you answered YES, then let it go. HINT: Deciding to let it go does not mean it is OK that it happened, just that you are deciding not to carry the sadness with you.

WORKSHEET 3.6: Exploring Emotions in Your Difficult Experience:

FEAR or ANXIETY

Please choose which Exploring Emotions in Your Difficult Experience sheet/s (Worksheets 3.5 to 3.8) you want to review after each 20- to 30-minute difficult experience writing exercise (Worksheet 3.2) OR difficult experience daily review (Worksheet 3.4). Complete this worksheet once weekly and review it with each daily review. If you need more space for any question, just grab a sheet of paper and keep writing.

1. What are you afraid of or anxious about? _____

_____

2. What is the actual threat now? _____

_____

3. Are you more anxious or afraid than you think most people would be?

     YES   NO   I AM NOT SURE

If you answered YES, why do you think you may be more afraid or anxious than others are?

_____

_____

If you answered NO or I AM NOT SURE, describe below what you need to do to protect yourself. If you cannot think of anything, then the fear may be more than it needs to be now.

_____

_____

4. Are you ready to let the fear and anxiety go?

     YES   NO   I AM NOT SURE

If you answered NO or I AM NOT SURE, what do you need to be ready to let the fear or anxiety go? HINT: Only YOU can decide when to let the fear or anxiety go. _____

_____

If you answered YES, then let it go. HINT: Deciding to let it go does not mean it is OK that it happened, just that you are deciding not to carry the fear and anxiety with you.

WORKSHEET 3.7: Exploring Emotions in Your Difficult Experience:

ANGER

Please choose which Exploring Emotions in Your Difficult Experience sheet/s (Worksheets 3.5 to 3.8) you want to review after each 20- to 30-minute difficult experience writing exercise (Worksheet 3.2) OR difficult experience daily review (Worksheet 3.4). Complete this worksheet once weekly and review it with each daily review. If you need more space for any question, just grab a sheet of paper and keep writing.

1. What are you angry, frustrated, or resentful about? _____

_____

_____

2. Holding on to anger can keep you stuck in the memory and feeling like a victim rather than a survivor. This is true even when you may have good reasons to be angry at someone or something that happened. Are you ready to let the anger/frustration/resentment go?

      YES   NO   I AM NOT SURE

If you answered NO or I AM NOT SURE, what do you need to be ready to let the anger/frustration/resentment go? HINT: Only YOU can decide when to let the anger go.

_____

_____

If you answered YES, then let it go. HINT: Deciding to let it go does not mean it is OK that it happened, just that you are deciding not to carry the anger, frustration, or resentment with you.

WORKSHEET 3.8: Exploring Emotions in Your Difficult Experience:

GUILT

Please choose which Exploring Emotions in Your Difficult Experience sheet/s (Worksheets 3.5 to 3.8) you want to review after each 20- to 30-minute difficult experience writing exercise (Worksheet 3.2) OR difficult experience daily review (Worksheet 3.4). Complete this worksheet once weekly and review it with each daily review. If you need more space for any question, just grab a sheet of paper and keep writing.

1. What do you feel guilty about from the difficult experience? _____

_____

_____

2. Holding on to guilt can keep you stuck in the memory and feeling responsible for something you could not control. Are you ready to let the guilt go?

     YES   NO   I AM NOT SURE

If you answered YES, then let it go. HINT: Deciding to let it go does not mean it is OK that it happened, just that you are deciding not to carry the guilt with you any longer.

If you answered NO or I AM NOT SURE, what do you need to do to be ready to let the guilt go? When a situation turns out badly, we all wish we could have done something to have it turn out better.

3. What percentage was your responsibility? HINT: Only YOU can decide when to let the guilt go.

_____

_____

4. If you wish you had done something differently, why didn't you? What aspects of the difficult experience context impacted the choices you made at the time? Even if you were partly responsible for what happened, did the situation or anyone else also have some responsibility? _____

_____

_____

5. If your family member, loved one, or friend came to you to talk about feeling guilty about a difficult experience like what you went through, what would you say to them? _____

_____

_____

MEMORY EXPOSURE AND PROCESSING EXAMPLE:
DAVID, THE ICU NURSE

Here is a specific example of memory exposure and processing using the example of David, who you first met in Chapter 1.

As things began to get worse, David decided to try the *Making Meaning of Difficult Experiences* workbook as a way to help with the impact of his intense work life. When David got to the section on memory processing, he slowed down and took his time. The first task is to think through which memory is impacting us the most now. Usually if we think about the past 2 weeks and which memory has taken up most of our thoughts and energy, that can be a good place to start. (As mentioned earlier, if more than one memory is causing you trouble and these memories seem pretty equal, just pick one to get started.) David decided to work on the memory of Clem's death. Clem was a man in his late 70s who arrived in the ER due to difficulty breathing. After arriving at the hospital, he was found to be positive for COVID-19. While Clem's stay was only for a few days, David connected with him and spent time with him, especially since Clem was not allowed visitors due to pandemic rules. His condition deteriorated quickly over 3 days, leading to his death as his lungs gave out. While Clem died more than 3 months ago, David still regularly had images of the whole medical team providing an intervention to try to remove lung fluid right before Clem died.

As illustrated in Figures 3.1 to 3.11, David completed the memory exercise focused on that difficult experience.

WORKSHEET 3.1: Mood Thermometers

Date: 06/18/2020

Make a mark on each line that describes how you have been feeling on *average* over the *past week*. We suggest you complete a new version of this worksheet once per week while working on the program.

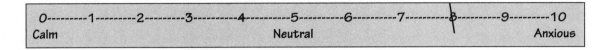

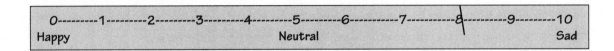

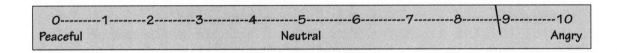

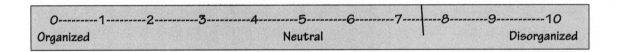

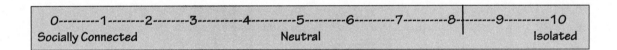

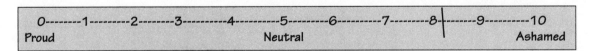

FIGURE 3.1 DAVID'S COMPLETED MOOD THERMOMETERS (FIRST TIME) (WORKSHEET 3.1)

WORKSHEET 3.2: Difficult Experience Writing Exercise

Date: _06/18/2020_

> Rate your distress right BEFORE completing the difficult experience exercise:
>
> 0--------1--------2---------3---------4---------5----------6-----------7----------8-----------9----------10
> Completely Relaxed   Noticeably Upset   Most Distressed Ever

Describe your difficult experience below. Begin from the moment in the memory when you feel it getting difficult or messy and end at the moment when you feel the immediate risk or event is over. Include all the details that let you connect with the memory including what you see, what you feel in your body, what you think, and how the details unfold. Let yourself feel the emotions as they come up. Do not avoid or push them away. Revisit the memory by writing in the present tense as though it is happening now. When you finish writing it out once, review it twice or for 20 to 30 minutes, whichever is longer. Please feel free to use additional pages.

Gary comes by to tell me that a team just ran to Clem's room due to his SpO2 dropping to 70. I rush to make it. I know he is not doing well. He was intubated and put on a ventilator last night and I thought then that he would likely pass away over the next few days. His lips are blue and he is not awake anymore. He has an DNR in place at this point. I just got off a call with his daughter about 10 minutes ago and told her that I am sorry but there is no way for her to visit her father due to Covid-19 protocols. I am feeling terrible saying this to her, as she is practically begging to be with her dad. I am convinced he is not likely to survive another day. We plan to have a video call by phone later this night despite Clem not being awake. His daughter just wants to see him once more. When I get to Clem's room, it does not look good. The team is working to try to increase his oxygen yet it keeps dipping lower. He was intubated already but his oxygenation was still dipping. The team is trying to increase oxygen flow. NO success. He is not getting the oxygen he needs, and I am horrified that I can do nothing more. This kind old man who I had read to last night is going to be another pandemic casualty. I am panicking on the inside but do not want to show it. I'm feeling my heart pounding and my stomach so tight I am nauseous, and it feels like I can't catch my breath. The medical team is rushing around but with a DNR, we really don't have much to do. I hold Clem's hand. After about 10 minutes of scrambling, Angela yells "V-tach," and Clem is gone, and with DNR in place the team stops. All of the medical team lock eyes in frustration over another patient death. I have tears in my eyes that I don't want the others to see. We pause and Dr. Anderson says to note the time of death as 20:30. I feel the tension leave my body and deep sadness take over. I hate the thought of calling his daughter and telling her Clem had died.

How long did you work on the difficult experience exercise? _30_ **minutes**

> Rate your distress right AFTER completing the difficult experience exercise:
>
> 0--------1--------2---------3---------4---------5----------6-----------7----------8-----------9----------10
> Completely Relaxed   Noticeably Upset   Most Distressed Ever

> Rate the HIGHEST level of your distress during the difficult experience exercise:
>
> 0--------1--------2---------3---------4---------5----------6-----------7----------8---------9---------10
> Completely Relaxed   Noticeably Upset   Most Distressed Ever

Review Worksheet 3.2: Difficult Experience Writing Exercise, at least three times per week or even daily if you would like. For each review, read the memory at least three times or for at least 20 to 30 minutes and complete a record of your review using Worksheet 3.4: Daily Review of the Difficult Experiences Writing Exercise.

FIGURE 3.2 DAVID'S COMPLETED DIFFICULT EXPERIENCE WRITING EXERCISE (FIRST TIME WRITING) (WORKSHEET 3.2)

WORKSHEET 3.3: Difficult Experience Processing Exercise

Please review the processing questions after each 20- to 30-minute difficult experience writing exercise (Worksheet 3.2) OR difficult experience daily review (Worksheet 3.4) and complete this worksheet once weekly. If you need more space for any question, just grab a sheet of paper and keep writing.

1. Why did this happen to you? What was the cause? *Because people do not care about others, and they will not do simple things like wear masks.*

2. How did the difficult experience change how you think about yourself? *I felt helpless and used up. I wonder if I can do this anymore.*

3. How did the difficult experience change how you think about others? *People are so irresponsible. If more people would just wear masks, get vaccinated, and quarantine, we might get through this and quit having the most vulnerable people paying for the selfish people who will not follow guidelines.*

4. How did the difficult experience change how you see the world? *People do not take care of each other enough. They are selfish. The world sucks right now.*

5. After completing Worksheets 3.2 or 3.4, what new, different, or important information did you notice today? *I had not thought about how Clem was struggling in that moment. I also did not remember how he seemed to relax a bit when I picked up his hand even though he was sedated. He seemed to relax when he heard my voice. I couldn't save his life, but at least he knew I was with him. He didn't die alone. His daughter found comfort in this when I spoke with her.*

6. What would you tell your family member, loved one, or friend if this had happened to them? *You did your job and were with Clem to the end. You can't save everyone, but you did your best for him and were with him.*

FIGURE 3.3 DAVID'S COMPLETED DIFFICULT EXPERIENCE PROCESSING EXERCISE (FIRST TIME) (WORKSHEET 3.3)

Based on his difficult experience, David chose to explore the emotion of sadness for the first week. Review the example worksheet figures below to see how he explored this emotion.

WORKSHEET 3.5: Exploring Emotions in Your Difficult Experience:

SADNESS

Please choose which Exploring Emotions in Your Difficult Experience sheet/s (Worksheets 3.5 to 3.8) you want to review after each 20- to 30-minute difficult experience writing exercise (Worksheet 3.2) OR difficult experience daily review (Worksheet 3.4). Complete this worksheet once weekly and review it with each daily review. If you need more space for any question, just grab a sheet of paper and keep writing.

1. Do you feel like this sadness is similar to how most people would be feeling at this point since the event?   YES   (NO)   I AM NOT SURE

If you answered YES, letting yourself grieve this loss or situation makes sense. Letting yourself feel sadness can often be the best way to move through sadness to the other side. What can you do to care for yourself while you grieve? _____

_____

If you answered NO or I AM NOT SURE, why do you think this level of sadness is sticking with you? *Because I really connected with Clem and felt he was a lot like my Dad would have been if he survived cancer. I really wanted Clem to make it through and spent time with him and connected with his daughter. Also, I felt like I was not really able to medically help him.*

Are you ready to let the sadness go? YES   NO   (I AM NOT SURE)

If you answered NO or I AM NOT SURE, what do you need to be ready to let the sadness go? HINT: Only YOU can decide when to let the sadness go. *I am really not sure, and I think I need more time to sit with this memory. I feel some relief, but I am not quite there.*

If you answered YES, then let it go. HINT: Deciding to let it go does not mean it is OK that it happened, just that you are deciding not to carry the sadness with you.

FIGURE 3.4 DAVID'S COMPLETED EXPLORING EMOTIONS IN YOUR DIFFICULT EXPERIENCE: SADNESS (FIRST TIME) (WORKSHEET 3.5)

WORKSHEET 3.4: Daily Review of the Difficult Experience Writing Exercise

Review Worksheet 3.2: Difficult Experience Writing Exercise, at least three times per week or even daily if you would like. For each review, read the memory at least three times or for at least 20 to 30 minutes and complete a record of your review using this Worksheet to record your distress just prior to, during, and just after each difficult experience daily review. Remember, we suggest that each difficult experience daily review includes

1. Reading the difficult memory from the Difficult Experience Writing Exercise (Worksheet 3.2) at least three times or for 20 minutes—whichever is longer.
2. Completing a Difficult Experience Processing Exercise once per week or reviewing this week's version (Worksheet 3.3).
3. Completing your choice of the Exploring Emotions in Your Difficult Experience (Worksheets 3.5 to 3.8) once per week or reviewing this week's version.

Use the following scale to rate your distress:

0--------1---------2--------3----------4----------5---------6----------7---------8----------9---------10
Completely   Mostly   Noticeably   Very   Most Upset
Relaxed   Relaxed   Upset   Upset   Ever

Date of review	Minutes reviewed	Distress level right **BEFORE** reviewing the difficult experience (0–10)	Distress level right **AFTER** reviewing the difficult experience (0–10)	**HIGHEST** level of distress reviewing the difficult experience (0–10)
06/19/2020	20	7	5	7
06/20/2020	30	5	4	5
06/22/2020	30	5	2	5
06/23/2020	30	2	2	3
06/24/2020	30	2	1	2
06/25/2020	30	2	1	2

FIGURE 3.5 DAVID'S COMPLETED DAILY REVIEW OF THE DIFFICULT EXPERIENCE WRITING EXERCISE (FIRST TIME) (WORKSHEET 3.4)

WORKSHEET 3.1: Mood Thermometers

Date: _06/25/2020_

Make a mark on each line that describes how you have been feeling on *average* over the *past week*. We suggest you complete a new version of this worksheet once per week while working on the program.

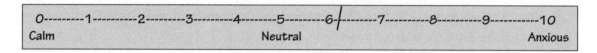

0---------1----------2---------3--------4-------5--------6-|--------7---------8----------9-----------10
Calm   Neutral   Anxious

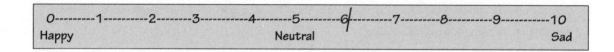

0---------1----------2--------3----------4--------5---------6|--------7--------8--------9----------10
Happy   Neutral   Sad

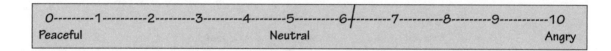

0---------1----------2--------3---------4-------5----------6|--------7---------8--------9-----------10
Peaceful   Neutral   Angry

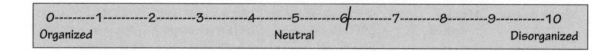

0---------1----------2--------3----------4--------5--------6|--------7---------8--------9-----------10
Organized   Neutral   Disorganized

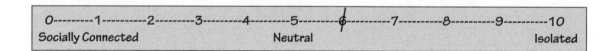

0---------1----------2-------3--------4--------5--------6|--------7--------8----------9---------10
Socially Connected   Neutral   Isolated

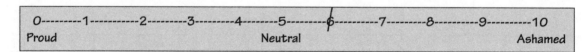

0---------1----------2--------3---------4-------5--------6|--------7--------8----------9---------10
Proud   Neutral   Ashamed

FIGURE 3.6 DAVID'S COMPLETED MOOD THERMOMETERS (SECOND TIME) (WORKSHEET 3.1)

WORKSHEET 3.2: Difficult Experience Writing Exercise

Date: _06/25/2020_

> Rate your distress right BEFORE completing the difficult experience exercise:
>
> 0---------1---------2--------3--------(4)-------5---------6----------7--------8---------9----------10
>
> Completely Relaxed   Noticeably Upset   Most Distressed Ever

Describe your difficult experience below. Begin from the moment in the memory when you feel it getting difficult or messy and end at the moment when you feel the immediate risk or event is over. Include all the details that let you connect with the memory, including what you see, what you feel in your body, what you think, and how the details unfold. Let yourself feel the emotions as they come up. Do not avoid or push them away. Revisit the memory by writing in the present tense as though it is happening now. When you finish writing it out once, review it twice or for 20 to 30 minutes, whichever is longer. Please feel free to use additional pages.

Clem's daughter is very upset that she cannot see her father and he is dying. She is comforted that I am with him and attending to his needs as much as I can given the crazy chaos in the hospital. I update her that he has been on a ventilator since last night and continues to worsen. I let her know that earlier in the week I had been reading his favorite book to him when I went on break and he really enjoyed it. I am hanging up the phone with Clem's daughter when Gary pops his head in to say Clem's oxygen is crashing. I am running to his room. I know he will likely die soon, and I am hoping he can make it to the evening call I plan to make with his daughter. She knows her father is not responsive but she wants to just see him again even just laying there. When I get to Clem's room, his lips are blue and his hand is cold when I touch it. The team is trying to increase oxygen flow but his oxygenation remains low despite all they try to do. He is not getting the oxygen he needs and I am horrified that I cannot do anything. I feel totally helpless. I am holding his hand and he seems to relax just a little bit even though he is not really conscious due to sedation. He has a DNR so we all know this is probably the end. I speak slowly and calmly to him even though he is not awake. I am panicking on the inside but do not want to show it. The medical team is rushing around to increase the ventilation. After about 10 minutes of scrambling, Angela yells "V-tach" and Clem is dead. All of the medical team locks eyes in frustration for another patient dying from Covid. I have tears in my eyes. We pause and Dr. Anderson is saying to note the time of death as 20:30. I feel the tension leave my body and deep sadness take over.

How long did you work on the difficult experience exercise? _30_ **minutes**

> Rate your distress right AFTER completing the difficult experience exercise:
>
> 0---------1---------2--------3-------(4)-------5---------6----------7--------8---------9----------10
>
> Completely Relaxed   Noticeably Upset   Most Distressed Ever

> Rate the HIGHEST level of your distress during the difficult experience exercise:
>
> 0---------1---------2--------3-------(4)-------5---------6----------7--------8---------9----------10
>
> Completely Relaxed   Noticeably Upset   Most Distressed Ever

Review Worksheet 3.2: Difficult Experience Writing Exercise, at least three times per week or even daily if you would like. For each review, read the memory at least three times or for at least 20 to 30 minutes and complete a record of your review using Worksheet 3.4: Daily Review of the Difficult Experiences Writing Exercise.

FIGURE 3.7 DAVID'S COMPLETED DIFFICULT EXPERIENCE WRITING EXERCISE (SECOND TIME WRITING) (WORKSHEET 3.2)

WORKSHEET 3.3: Difficult Experience Processing Exercise

Please review the processing questions after each 20- to 30-minute difficult experience writing exercise (Worksheet 3.2) OR difficult experience daily review (Worksheet 3.4) and complete this worksheet weekly. If you need more space for any question, just grab a sheet of paper and keep writing.

1. Why did this happen to you? What was the cause? *Because this pandemic is dangerous and we do not yet have a way to save everyone. Also, I connect to my patients and care about them. This was especially hard and it happened more quickly than any of us had expected.*

2. How did the difficult experience change how you think about yourself? *I felt helpless and in that moment I felt exhausted. Talking through it is helping me to see that I can have a role in comforting even when I cannot save someone, and that role is also important.*

3. How did the difficult experience change how you think about others? *I am angry with people who do not do simple things to protect vulnerable others, like wearing masks.*

4. How did the difficult experience change how you see the world? *The pandemic sucks. There is no one who is not affected by it.*

5. After completing Worksheets 3.2 or 3.4, what new, different, or important information did you notice today? *Today I was really impacted by remembering that Clem seemed to relax when I held his hand. I know he was not conscious, but I feel like somehow he knew I was there while he died. It can be important to not be alone when you die, and I had the chance to be that for Clem. It helped his daughter, too, knowing he didn't die alone.*

6. What would you tell your family member, loved one, or friend if this had happened to them? *You did your job and were with Clem to the end.*

FIGURE 3.8 DAVID'S COMPLETED DIFFICULT EXPERIENCE PROCESSING EXERCISE (SECOND TIME) (WORKSHEET 3.3)

WORKSHEET 3.4: Daily Review of the Difficult Experience Writing Exercise

Review Worksheet 3.2: Difficult Experience Writing Exercise, at least three times per week or even daily if you would like. For each review, read the memory at least three times or for at least 20 to 30 minutes and complete a record of your review using this Worksheet to record your distress just prior to, during, and just after each difficult experience daily review. Remember, we suggest that each difficult experience daily review includes

1. Reading the difficult memory from the Difficult Experience Writing Exercise (Worksheet 3.2) at least three times or 20 minutes—whichever is longer.
2. Completing a Difficult Experience Processing Exercise (Worksheet 3.3) once per week or reviewing this week's version.
3. Completing your choice of the Exploring Emotions in Your Difficult Experience (Worksheets 3.5 to 3.8) once per week or reviewing this week's version.

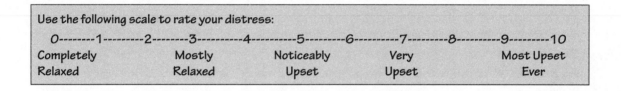

Use the following scale to rate your distress:

0--------1---------2--------3----------4----------5---------6----------7---------8----------9---------10
Completely Relaxed   Mostly Relaxed   Noticeably Upset   Very Upset   Most Upset Ever

Date of REVIEW	Minutes reviewed	Distress level right BEFORE reviewing the difficult experience (0–10)	Distress level right AFTER reviewing the difficult experience (0–10)	HIGHEST level of distress reviewing the difficult experience (0–10)
06/26/2020	30	4	2	4
06/27/2020	30	1	1	1
06/29/2020	30	1	0	1
06/30/2020	20	0	0	0

FIGURE 3.9 DAVID'S COMPLETED DAILY REVIEW OF THE DIFFICULT EXPERIENCE WRITING EXERCISE (SECOND TIME) (WORKSHEET 3.4)

WORKSHEET 3.5: Exploring Emotions in Your Difficult Experience:

SADNESS

Please choose which Exploring Emotions in Your Difficult Experience sheet/s (Worksheets 3.5 to 3.8) you want to review after each 20- to 30-minute difficult experience writing exercise (Worksheet 3.2) OR difficult experience daily review (Worksheet 3.4). Complete this worksheet weekly and review it with each daily review. If you need more space for any question, just grab a sheet of paper and keep writing.

1. Do you feel like this sadness is similar to how most people would be feeling at this point since the event?   YES   NO   I AM NOT SURE

If you answered YES, letting yourself grieve this loss or situation makes sense. Letting yourself feel sadness can often be the best way to move through sadness to the other side. What can you do to care for yourself while you grieve? _____

_____

If you answered NO or I AM NOT SURE, why do you think this level of sadness is sticking with you?

Because I connected with Clem and his family and I wanted to help.

Are you ready to let the sadness go?   YES   NO   I AM NOT SURE

If you answered NO or I AM NOT SURE, what do you need to be ready to let the sadness go? HINT: Only YOU can decide when to let the sadness go. _____

_____

If you answered YES, then let it go. HINT: Deciding to let it go does not mean it is OK that it happened, just that you are deciding not to carry the sadness with you.

FIGURE 3.10 DAVID'S COMPLETED EXPLORING EMOTIONS IN YOUR DIFFICULT EXPERIENCE: SADNESS (SECOND TIME) (WORKSHEET 3.5)

WORKSHEET 3.1: Mood Thermometers

Date: 07/02/2020

Make a mark on each line that describes how you have been feeling on *average* over the *past week*. We suggest you complete a new version of this worksheet once per week while working on the program.

0---------1---------2---------3---------4---------5---------6--------7---------8---------9----------10
Calm   Neutral   Anxious

0---------1---------2---------3---------4---------5---------6--------7---------8---------9---------10
Happy   Neutral   Sad

0---------1---------2---------3---------4---------5---------6--------7---------8---------9----------10
Peaceful   Neutral   Angry

0---------1---------2---------3---------4---------5---------6--------7--------8---------9---------10
Organized   Neutral   Disorganized

0---------1---------2---------3---------4---------5---------6--------7--------8---------9----------10
Socially Connected   Neutral   Isolated

0---------1---------2---------3---------4---------5---------6--------7---------8---------9----------10
Proud   Neutral   Ashamed

FIGURE 3.11 DAVID'S COMPLETED MOOD THERMOMETERS (LAST TIME) (WORKSHEET 3.1)

As you can see from the completed worksheets, David's work approaching the difficult experience was not easy. He felt some strong feelings as he first approached Clem's death. He stuck with it. As he approached the memory by writing it out and reading it in review sessions, the intensity of those emotions got less over time—as you see in the reduction in distress ratings. The ratings went down both during each time he stayed with it for 30 minutes and across the reviews he completed as he worked on the difficult experience. In addition, David had some important new thoughts about what he did at the time of Clem's death and after.

He decided that he wanted to focus his work on sadness and completed the sadness worksheet twice. He really thought about the experience over and over again and gave himself room to think about it differently. David considered how his presence with Clem before his death (reading to him in the hospital and his connection with Clem's daughter) impacted Clem, the family, and himself. David also was able to consider this differently over time. He was able to be a part of Clem's daughter's healing process because he cared for her dad. David noticed that as he started to think about Clem's death, it was no longer stuck in his head. He thought about it less at other times of the day and when he was trying to fall asleep. He was feeling less burned out at work and more able to connect with people again. As his feelings of burnout lifted, he was able to make progress in other areas as well.

CHAPTER 4

Getting Active

CATCHING UP WITH OUR CASE EXAMPLES

Ann

As we discussed in earlier chapters, Ann—who had been sexually assaulted at a club—isolated herself. She only went back and forth to work and avoided restrooms with more than one stall. But since her friend Samantha had given her a copy of this workbook and offered to help, Ann worked with Samantha on some of her goals to become more active. She started by asking Samantha to have dinner, which went well, so she asked if they could have dinner together once a week, which Samantha was happy to accept. Ann used to attend yoga classes twice per week prior to the assault and decided to add yoga back to her routine. She asked Samantha to attend yoga with her the first time, then felt OK attending on her own. Ann used to enjoy grocery shopping after work but hadn't been inside a grocery store (or anywhere else) since the assault, so she decided to go to her favorite grocery store after work. Gradually, Ann added back in the activities that she had stopped after the assault. The hardest activity for her was to go back to that club. She asked Samantha and a few of their friends to go dancing at that same club one Saturday night. Samantha obviously knew about the assault, but their other friends did not. Ann was understandably nervous at first but was able to dance and have fun with her friends. She felt she had reclaimed this club as a place she could go.

David

Remember David, the ICU nurse who cared for COVID-19 patients during the pandemic? He was so exhausted that he stopped exercising, wasn't eating properly, and was socially isolated. During his little time off, he was drinking too much and not sleeping. There was so much to be done and so many patients to be helped, and he felt he was in a downward spiral. After he started using the *Making Meaning of Difficult Experiences* program, David quickly saw some changes. Later you will read about his first effort to get active by dog sitting. In addition, his friend Angela had checked in with him because she saw his exhaustion and burnout and was worried. David opened up to her, and she quickly agreed to help him in any way she could. Angela picked up a copy of the workbook and started working on her own difficult experience. Together they supported each other to get back into their good coping skills that had worked before. They restarted a regular Saturday bike ride in the park and talked with each other about their goals, including reducing alcohol consumption. David even decided to add more vegetables and fruits into his diet and cut out sugary snacks that he had been eating more of since the pandemic. All of these gradual changes really helped David to feel better about himself and connect with Angela and his other friends. He no longer felt like the only person fighting against the pandemic.

Miguel

When Miguel got home from the hospital after his deployment, his family was so happy to have him home. They had prepared the house for his return based on the suggestions of the rehabilitation case manager. Lisa and the kids were very excited to see him, but Miguel felt immediately overwhelmed by the people and attention, and he retreated to his space in the garage. Lisa and the girls, Gabriella and Maria, were sad that he did not want to spend time with them. He would only come out of the garage for work and meals and to watch football games. When he did join the family, Miguel was angry and his face was puffy from crying and drinking. Lisa invited a few of his military friends over for a playoff football game. Miguel had agreed to this visit, but on the day of the game he smiled only a little, barely talked to anyone, and drank too much.

Miguel avoided his family, his military friends, and going out. This avoidance was so severe that it was making his depression and drinking worse. Avoidance of the memory and of the people, places, and situations related to the improvised explosive device (IED) incident left Miguel stuck and sad. While his military buddies reminded him of the incident, he avoided his family because he felt guilty for his temper and problems since he returned. His VA provider worked with him to start to get active again as part of his posttraumatic stress disorder (PTSD) treatment. At first, getting back out there was hard. Some of the activities even brought up the memory of the IED, but Miguel quickly saw that as he stuck with it, it got easier, and pretty soon he was able to enjoy being with his family and friends and doing activities, like going to baseball games, again. After Miguel finished prolonged exposure therapy for PTSD, he decided to keep working on his difficult experience of the IED memory on his own with the *Making Meaning of Difficult Experiences* program. Below you will see a specific way he worked on getting active with his family.

GETTING ACTIVE: WHAT IS BEHAVIORAL ACTIVATION?

Behavioral activation essentially means getting and staying active. Behavioral activation is a way to increase your activities, which will hopefully improve your mood. Activating behaviors will activate better moods.

We need to take care of ourselves before we can take care of others. Part of this self-care is staying active and doing things that nourish our souls. When we are stressed or sad or recovering from a difficult situation, it is easy to put those activities aside, but then we aren't functioning at our best. Self-care activities include gardening, hiking, praying, meditating, reading, playing an instrument, going out with friends, going to art or music events, and seeing a movie with a friend. While some of these activities may be expensive or risky due to COVID-19, look for activities for you to do that are relatively safe in your current environment and that can fit into your budget. It can be helpful to put these activities on your calendar (for example, take a walk on Wednesday at 10:00 AM) and schedule them with other people (for example, meet Jenna for dinner at 7:30 PM at the Thai place we like). At a very basic level, take medications as prescribed, eat healthily, shower or bathe, brush your teeth, and take care of work and household chores each day.

Even when—and maybe especially when—we are sad or hurt or recovering from a difficult situation, we need to stay active. The law of inertia states: *Objects at rest tend to stay at rest; objects in motion tend to stay in motion.* The longer you are inactive, the harder it becomes to get active, and if fear or sadness is added to that mix, it can be paralyzing.

As is the case throughout *Making Meaning of Difficult Experiences*, it is your choice what to work on and you can track your goals and progress on the worksheets in this workbook. If your activity level is where you want it to be, you can skip this chapter. If you think this reminder to stay active and schedule enjoyable activities is sufficient to get you where you need to be, feel free to move on as well. However, if you are not as active as you would like to be or as active as you think would be good for you, let's work on it! This work may be as simple as setting an intention and making a plan. Or it may not be that simple. You may have to break activities up into little steps that are easier to accomplish.

David

David knew he needed to make some changes. He reluctantly agreed to dog-sit Carlos's dog for a week. Carlos was an ICU respiratory therapist who was also burned out from the pandemic. He was going to visit his parents for the first time since the start of the pandemic. David knew once he agreed to dog-sit, he couldn't go back on his word, and he thought the accountability would be good for him.

Carlos dropped off Lucy, the cutest spaniel David had ever seen. She was shy at first, but quickly warmed up to David and played with him and cuddled in his lap and let him rub her belly. He spent time playing with Lucy and walking her, even taking her for longer walks on a trail in midtown. As soon as he got off a shift, David took care of Lucy instead of drinking. He enjoyed walking with her and found that he perked up getting outside and being more active.

We aren't saying that you have to commit to adopting or sitting for a pet, but anything that will get you up and moving helps. Accountability to another person or an animal helps to get us going even when we don't feel like it. Being physically active and getting outdoors are particularly helpful. Many people have found during the pandemic that going outside really boosts their mood. A change of scenery can nourish your mind and get you out of the habit of sitting on the couch and focusing on all the things you wish were better in your life.

David

Even after David gave Lucy back to Carlos, David was able to continue being more physically active, and he noticed the benefits. He would walk outside or in the hospital hallways for 15 minutes during a break and felt more energetic for the rest of his shift. He started monitoring his steps. He continued to take Lucy for longer walks on the trail on his days off when Carlos let Lucy visit. He made plans with friends for COVID-safe meals together and outdoor activities. Lucy had helped to jump-start David's becoming active, but he saw the benefits and continued to stay active.

ASSESSING YOUR ACTIVITIES

Using Worksheet 4.1: Your List of Daily Activities, write down the activities you did each day this past week. This worksheet is located near the end of this chapter and also can be found in Appendix A near the end of this workbook. For an example of how David filled out his List of Daily Activities, look at Figure 4.1: David's Completed List of Daily Activities (Worksheet 4.1).

How does your list of activities look? Are you satisfied with how active you are? Are you getting the basics done, such as work and household chores and basic hygiene? Now let's look at your plan for next week. On Worksheet 4.2: Your Action Plan, write down your plan. Start with your "must do" activities such as work and chores and basic hygiene for the coming week. Then

WORKSHEET 4.1: Your List of Daily Activities

Day	Activity
Monday	Ate lunch at favorite food truck with Jake
Tuesday	Watched TV
Wednesday	Read a book at home
Thursday	Went for walk around block after work and talked with Judy
Friday	Dinner with Jake; read before bed
Saturday	Laundry
Sunday	Went to church with Jake, walking trail with Judy

FIGURE 4.1 DAVID'S COMPLETED LIST OF DAILY ACTIVITIES (WORKSHEET 4.1)

add in some fun activities. The worksheet can be found near the end of this chapter and also in Appendix A. Please complete a new Worksheet 4.2: Your Action Plan every week. Multiple copies of this worksheet are included in Appendix A. Make sure you include both the basic activities that you have to do and activities that would feel good for you, be fun, and make you feel like you are living your best life right now. For an example of how David filled out his Action Plan, look at Figure 4.2: David's Completed Action Plan (Worksheet 4.2).

Now that you have seen what an Action Plan can look like if you are having trouble coming up with activities, check out Appendix B, "Suggestions for Pleasant Activities."

Looking at your first completed Worksheet 4.2: Your Action Plan, commit to what you want to do each day this coming week. Consider activities that may be low-cost or no-cost that you can do fairly often. The goal of this exercise is getting out to do the activity, not the cost of the activity or how special it is. We want to increase how much activity you do and how often you do it. You can consider including the occasional really special event—like an outdoor concert—but make sure you include some simple activities as well. You want to have things you can keep on doing and do over time. Building these habits of self-care is as important as working hard.

If you are having trouble completing Worksheet 4.2, keep reading this chapter to learn more about the skill of behavioral activation. Some people need more direction to get themselves activated, especially if they are feeling tired or blue.

WORKSHEET 4.2: Your Action Plan

Week 1: Write down your goals for this coming week: _Increase "me" time_

Day	Activity
Monday	Go for a walk on my own; visit with Andrew
Tuesday	Yoga
Wednesday	Try new mediation app
Thursday	Movie with Peggy
Friday	Relax and watch my favorite show and go for a walk on my own
Saturday	Lunch with Omar
Sunday	Go to church, have lunch with Omar and Jake, walking trail with Judy

Then after you have done something on your list, evaluate it:

How did it go? _I think I did ok. I ended up inviting my sister over because she had a tough day at work. We still relaxed._

How did you feel afterwards? _Happy that I was able to refocus for a bit and not always take care of others._

What do you want to try differently next time? _Different meditation app—I did not care for this one._

Do you want to do this activity again? __x__Yes _____No

What next? _Repeat the plan next week with different app._

FIGURE 4.2 DAVID'S COMPLETED ACTION PLAN (WORKSHEET 4.2)

GETTING STARTED

To get started working on behavioral activation, set a goal for yourself that is easy to achieve right away and every day, such as reading for pleasure at least 15 minutes per day or doing something social at least three times this week, and commit to it starting immediately. (Hint: do not include watching TV if you are just "vegging out.")

Sometimes it can help to invite a friend to do these enjoyable activities with you. This person can be an ally to talk with about the challenges of starting a new activity, and they can even make it more fun. You can provide support for one another and give each other tips for how to succeed. They can help keep you accountable even when you don't feel like doing the activity. Almost everyone tells us that they are happy they did their chosen activity, even if they had to drag themselves to it. In Chapter 5, we focus on social connection and sharing your difficult experience with others. Someone you are working with on getting active may also be someone with whom you can share your difficult experience memory.

You may need to start your behavioral activation plan with small steps. Do not go too big too fast! For example, if you haven't felt up to cleaning your place in a while, break that down into smaller steps that feel achievable, such as

- Wipe out the sink with damp toilet paper after brushing your teeth in the morning.
- Wipe around the sink area with damp toilet paper after brushing your teeth the next morning.
- Wipe one wall of the shower with wash cloth after you shower.
- Wipe two walls of the shower with wash cloth after you shower.
- Wipe area of floor around toilet with damp toilet paper.
- Use toilet bowl cleaner and brush to clean toilet on the weekend.
- Empty all trash cans.
- Take out the kitchen garbage.
- Sweep the kitchen, and so on.

What this means is don't write down the broad goal of "clean the house" on Worksheet 4.2: Your Action Plan if you haven't cleaned your house in 6 months. Be kind to yourself and forgiving. Maybe it didn't used to be a big deal for you to clean the house regularly before the difficult experience occurred, but accept that things are different now. You don't need to beat yourself up about what is hard for you now. If a friend were going through a hard time, you would likely be supportive and understand their need to work on small steps, so be gracious to yourself as well. If there are activities on your list that you want to do and intend to do and just can't seem to do, that is a clue that you need to break that activity down into smaller, more manageable steps. Once you get into the habit of doing your activities again, you may be able to include broader goals such as "clean the house."

Tips for Behavioral Activation

1. Stay active and do things that nourish your soul.
2. This can include gardening, hiking, praying, meditating, reading, playing an instrument, going out with friends, going to art or music events, and seeing a movie with a friend.
3. Look for activities that fit your budget and are relatively safe in your current environment, including the COVID-19 pandemic.
4. Put activities on your calendar.
5. Include other people whenever possible.
6. Always take the time to shower or bathe and take care of work and household chores each day.
7. Break activities down into manageable steps.

Good job! Monitoring something we are trying to change is the first step in making those changes. Getting active is how we start. Paying attention to how things go will help you do them in a way that is most helpful for you. And remember it is always OK to break tasks up into smaller, more achievable steps. Now you can use what you have learned here to keep up your new self-care habits and move on to improving your social connections in Chapter 5. Well done!

EXAMPLES OF APPLYING BEHAVIORAL ACTIVATION

Miguel: Re-engaging with His Family

Miguel was ready to really start being present with his family again. He decided to work on a behavioral activation plan. His first priority was his children. He wanted to be involved in Gabriella's and Maria's lives. He didn't have energy, and it seemed too overwhelming to even start, so Miguel asked Lisa for help. He was embarrassed about how long he had been isolated in the garage. He felt like a failure as a father.

Lisa knew just what to do. She set up a family game night. Prior to deployment, they always had at least one night a week when they would sit down to play games together. Miguel was on board as soon as Lisa suggested it. He even said they should start with Yahtzee because it was loud, and he wanted to really challenge himself to stay in a situation that was safe and loud. The next night, all four of them played Yahtzee for 2 hours. Miguel joked and laughed with his wife and daughters. He truly enjoyed the time, and Miguel felt like he was a father again.

Shaquila

Shaquila still felt very sad after her miscarriage. She dragged herself to work, didn't talk to anyone, came back home, and vegged out on the sofa mindlessly watching TV. This was her life now. Her wife,

Tanja, was sad, too, but seemed to be doing a better job of "going through the motions." After several months of what felt to Shaquila like a non-existence, she started the Making Meaning of Difficult Experiences program. She worked through the memory of the miscarriage using the memory processing skill (Chapter 3) and identified some thoughts that were probably not accurate (the miscarriage was her fault, this meant she would never have a baby, and Tanja was sorry she had agreed that Shaquila have a baby) and found memory processing very helpful. She decided that talking to her friends and family and other people who loved her was important, so she followed a plan to increase her social connection (to be covered in Chapter 5). She knew she wasn't taking care of herself as well as she should, so Shaquila worked on that when she reached Chapter 6 in the workbook.

In some ways, the behavioral activation skill was the easiest to work on because the couple had been very active previously, so Shaquila worked on adding back some of the activities she and Tanja used to enjoy. For example:

- Shaquila had loved to garden and was proud of her yard, but she hadn't touched it in almost a year. She had been so preoccupied with the process of getting pregnant, then feeling nauseous and tired, and then experiencing so much sadness after she lost the baby that her garden badly needed TLC. She went into the yard after work to assess the damage. The next day, Shaquila went back out after work and started raking the leaves and trash out of the garden. The day after that, she weeded. She worked on the garden a little bit each day, more on the weekends, and made a commitment to get it back into shape.
- Shaquila and Tanja re-engaged with their book club and started reading the book for the next meeting.
- Shaquila ordered take-out from their favorite restaurant and invited friends to eat in their backyard with them.
- Shaquila and Tanja talked to the fertility doctor about when it would be OK to start trying to get pregnant again.

None of this was easy for Shaquila. At first, she felt like she was having to drag herself through the process. She felt like she hardly remembered any of that first book and didn't add anything to the book club discussion. But gradually, as she kept up the activities, they got easier and she felt more engaged. Shaquila felt kind of like her garden, with both of them coming alive again, and she knew that both needed continued attention and maintenance even when—or especially when—hard things happened.

For an example of how Shaquila completed her Action Plan over the course of 6 weeks, look at Figure 4.3: Shaquila's Completed Action Plan (Worksheet 4.2).

As you can see in our case examples and as you use the program, getting active means getting out and engaging in your life. It means doing the things that matter to you. For each person, getting active will look different. As long as you are getting up and getting connected with the world, you are meeting the goals of this chapter. Now let's get active!

WORKSHEET 4.2: Your Action Plan

Week 1: Write down your goals for this coming week: <u>Work on garden</u>

Day	Activity
Monday	Go look at garden
Tuesday	Rake leaves out of garden
Wednesday	Weed garden
Thursday	Weed garden
Friday	Spend some time in garden
Saturday	Get some new plants for garden
Sunday	Plant some plants in garden

Then, after you have done something on your list, evaluate it:

How did it go? <u>very well</u>

How did you feel afterward? <u>better, happy, interested</u>

What do you want to try differently next time? <u>keep up the momentum without trying to do too much</u>

Do you want to do this activity again? <u> x </u>Yes <u>   </u>No

What next? <u>start planting</u>

Week 2: Goals for this coming week: <u>Start planting garden, book club</u>

Day	Activity
Monday	Text Mary about book club
Tuesday	Get book from library
Wednesday	Start reading book
Thursday	Read book
Friday	Read book
Saturday	Read book, plant some plants in garden
Sunday	Read book, plant some plants in garden

Week 3: Goals for this coming week: <u>Work on garden, read book, go to book club</u>

Day	Activity
Monday	Read book
Tuesday	Read book
Wednesday	Read book
Thursday	Go to book club with Tanja
Friday	Get take-out
Saturday	Get book from library, start reading book
Sunday	Read book, plant some plants in garden

FIGURE 4.3 SHAQUILA'S COMPLETED ACTION PLAN (WORKSHEET 4.2)

Week 4: Goals for this coming week: _Garden, read, go to book club, have friends over_

Day	Activity
Monday	Read book
Tuesday	Read book
Wednesday	Read book
Thursday	Go to book club with Tanja
Friday	Get take-out and have Denicia and Tammy over out back
Saturday	Get book from library, start reading, go to farmer's market
Sunday	Read book, plant some plants in garden

Week 5: Goals for this coming week: _Garden, book club, go out with friends, make doc appt_

Day	Activity
Monday	Call and make doctor's appointment
Tuesday	Read
Wednesday	Read, take cuttings to Denicia
Thursday	Make pasta dish to bring to book club with Tanja
Friday	Happy hour with friends after work
Saturday	Get book, read, farmer's market, make dinner for friends over
Sunday	Read, work in garden

Week 6: Goals for this coming week: _Garden, book club, friends, go to doc appt_

Day	Activity
Monday	Read, clean house
Tuesday	Read
Wednesday	Go to fertility doctor with Tanja
Thursday	Make cheese app to bring to book club with Tanja
Friday	Have friends over after work
Saturday	Get book, read, errands
Sunday	Read, brunch, work in garden

FIGURE 4.3 CONTINUED

WORKSHEET 4.1: Your List of Daily Activities

Day	Activity
Monday	
Tuesday	
Wednesday	
Thursday	
Friday	
Saturday	
Sunday	

WORKSHEET 4.2: Your Action Plan

Week 1: Write down your goals for this coming week: _____

Day	Activity
Monday	
Tuesday	
Wednesday	
Thursday	
Friday	
Saturday	
Sunday	

Then, after you have done something on your list, evaluate it:

How did it go?

_____

How did you feel afterward?

_____

What do you want to try differently next time?

_____

Do you want to do this activity again?   _____Yes   _____No

What next?

_____

Week 2: Goals for this coming week: _____

Day	Activity
Monday	
Tuesday	
Wednesday	
Thursday	
Friday	
Saturday	
Sunday	

Week 3: Goals for this coming week: _____

Day	Activity
Monday	
Tuesday	
Wednesday	
Thursday	
Friday	
Saturday	
Sunday	

Week 4: Goals for this coming week: _____

Day	Activity
Monday	
Tuesday	
Wednesday	
Thursday	
Friday	
Saturday	
Sunday	

Week 5: Goals for this coming week: _____

Day	Activity
Monday	
Tuesday	
Wednesday	
Thursday	
Friday	
Saturday	
Sunday	

Week 6: Goals for this coming week: _____

Day	Activity
Monday	
Tuesday	
Wednesday	
Thursday	
Friday	
Saturday	
Sunday	

CHAPTER 5

The Healing Power of Social Connection

CATCHING UP WITH OUR CASE EXAMPLES

Ann

Ann started working to improve her social connections as soon as she decided to tell her friend Samantha about the assault. Asking Samantha to have dinner weekly and talking to her honestly about what was going on, including her work on *Making Meaning of Difficult Experiences*, helped Ann feel supported and not so alone in her pain. With her behavioral activation goal of going out with friends to the club, she was starting to become more socially active again. As Ann returned to her yoga class, her yoga instructor, Robin, who was an old friend, let her know how happy she was to see her back in class. Ann set the social connection goal (discussed in this chapter) of engaging more with Robin after class and eventually decided to confide in Robin about the assault. Robin was very supportive and helped Ann feel she was not to blame and not so alone.

David

David had always been a very sociable person, and one of the reasons he knew he was burned out was his desire to not be around people. As you learned through his work getting active, David prioritized connecting with others in his getting active plan. He reconnected with Angela, his friend, coworker, and neighbor, and, through this connection, he really started to see his depression lift. Even just having someone he could swing by to talk with after a tough day made a huge difference. Angela knew about his difficult experience in the death of his patient, Clem. She was able to listen, and he valued her opinion on the situation.

Miguel

Miguel focused his work on getting active on reconnecting with his family. This increased his social connection and also spurred him to reconnect with some of his Army friends who he had not spoken with since his injury. He was nervous to make the call to Lt. Sophia Brown who was badly burned but survived the IED attack. He spent an afternoon digging up her parents' number since he was not sure where she lived. When he called, Lt. Brown's mother, Lucretia, answered and was very happy to hear his voice. Lucretia said that Sophia had been medically discharged after the incident due to the burns on her leg. Sophia had months of medical procedures and rehabilitation. She was now working as a quality improvement specialist and doing well. She gave him Sophia's number and said she would love to hear from him. Miguel was both nervous and happy that he reconnected and was taking steps to reconnect with his military friends.

HUMAN BEINGS ARE SOCIAL BEINGS

Our connections to other people often define how we view ourselves and our roles and expectations in life. We generally try to be good parents, children, siblings, friends, and workers. We live in a society of other people. We care about people, and we care what other people think about us. When we have a difficult experience, a normal response is to consider how those around us might think about what happened to us. Do we think that they would have reacted as we did or differently? Do we think that others may feel we did something wrong or blame us for what happened? Would they think we did everything possible and want to help us feel better or even take care of us after the difficult experience? These relationships and how we perceive them can have a big impact on whether the difficult experience gets stuck in our mind or gets integrated into our life story and we move on. Years of research and clinical experience have taught us that people who reach out for help and social connection following a difficult experience are less likely to have long-lasting mental health problems. We are people who need people.

Reaching out for social support is one of the best ways to manage difficult experiences. Unfortunately, when we are stressed, we often avoid other people. Avoiding people is even more common if we feel guilty or worried that others may blame us for part or all of what happened. No one likes to be judged, but sometimes we judge ourselves more harshly than others would judge us. We cannot know, in fact, how others would judge us without talking to them. Even if we are partly responsible for what happened, that doesn't mean we will be shunned. It is important to let people who care about you help you process the difficult experience.

NOT ALL SOCIAL CONNECTIONS ARE POSITIVE

In this chapter, we focus on the skill of social connection and how to reach out to others to engage with the healing power of social support. As we approach social connection, it is important to think about different types of social connection because not all social contacts are healing. As you work toward building social support, if you find that you are feeling worse after certain connections (for instance, if you feel that you are not being heard or that the person is unkind or judgmental), then it may be best to look for other social supports. In addition, if certain social connections are encouraging you to engage in unhelpful coping behaviors, like using substances, it may be good to limit that contact as well. *Having enough of the right kinds of social contacts to feel supported as you deal with stressful memories is important.* Reducing negative social connections from the wrong kinds of social contact is also important. In this chapter, we will help you get more socially connected to positive social supports as you work through this difficult experience.

WHAT IS POSITIVE SOCIAL CONNECTION?

We all differ in how much and what kinds of social connections work for us. Let's start by identifying what positive social connection may look like. At its core, *positive social connection* refers to contact with others who recharge your emotion and coping battery. Such connections feed your soul; they feel good and allow you to feel connected to the world and to others and to feel valued. These connections do not require a deep relationship. Sometimes a simple hello and a smile to your neighbor on the street as you walk by can provide a boost of social connection. Other times, having a deep conversation with your best friend or partner can create a new sense of understanding about the difficult experience itself. Letting yourself notice and enjoy these social connections in many different relationships can enhance your mood and help you feel more a part of the wider world. This connection is important because we tend to feel alone in our pain.

These deeper positive social connections require that the other person be open to listening, thoughtful, and nonjudgmental. The focus of healing social connection is on listening—not fixing or blaming. Sometimes those who are closest to us want to "fix" the difficult experience rather than simply be there as you are working through the memory. They may respond with, "you should have . . .," or "why didn't you . . .," or "if this happens again you can . . .," rather than simply being present with you to walk through the experience. If you notice that someone you are connecting with is trying to solve the difficult experience or explain why it will not happen again in a way that you are not feeling heard, it may make sense to stop the discussion and let them know that right now you just want to be heard and do not want them to fix it. Perhaps this person doesn't know what to do to help, and this is their way of trying. If you can give them the benefit of the doubt, you could say something like, "I love that you are trying to fix this for me, but right now, all I need you to do is listen." In fact, it is often useful to start off the conversation with what you would like from the other person, such as, "I'm going to tell you what happened, and right now, all I need you to do is listen." If that does not work, you can try either with another person or on another day.

Social support is one of the most powerful healers and can be as simple as spending time with someone or it can involve deeper conversations. Social support helps you feel less alone in your pain and can offer a different perspective. It lets you know that people care. It can help you feel valued and loved, especially after a difficult experience that you feel guilty about. You want to pick people who can be supportive when you tell them about the difficult experience. If they are judgmental, you won't feel supported. Getting social support usually means talking to more than one person.

The more often you approach your difficult experience, the easier it will get for you to share the details. Some people may be better at hearing all of the messy memory, whereas others may only be able to hear less intense details. Consider what "version" of the memory you want to share as you consider beginning a social connection with someone. Is this a person who you want to know *all* the details? Most often we suggest reserving the whole story for those you most trust and those you feel confident will be compassionate with your memory, such as a close sibling or a spouse or a trusted friend. You may also share a less detailed version or a "just the facts" version with others, maybe colleagues or other friends, to let them know what you are going through but with less expectation that they will walk through the healing process with you.

CAREFULLY CONSIDER WHO CAN HELP

When you reach out to someone, consider that they may also have experienced difficult events in their past—events that may influence whether they are able to provide a helpful response or that may prevent them from listening to you. Remember that we only know what people share with us and that is often just a piece of their life experience. It can be helpful to disengage from unhelpful social connections and have compassion for those people who may not be able to provide support.

Some people are truly not able to provide the support that you need. It may be disappointing, but this does not say anything about you or how much the person cares about you. Accept the fact that they can't provide the type of social support you need right now. It's a bit like someone declining an invitation to play tennis with you because they don't know how to play tennis. If it isn't in their repertoire, you would do better to try to find someone who knows how to play and is available rather than being upset that they won't play with you. There are people available who *can* provide what you need, even if you are not feeling that way right now.

It is also true that sometimes people don't know how to respond, and they may say the wrong thing without meaning to. If you feel that their intentions are good, you may have to learn to forgive them and move on to someone else for the kind of support you need right now. You may have to try a few people until you find those who can provide what you need, and that's OK.

GETTING STARTED

As you approach your difficult experience, we encourage you to tell at least one person the whole story. It sounds different when you say it out loud rather than keeping it in your head. We feel strongly that it is inherently healing to tell someone who is trying to be helpful about the worst moments of your life. In fact, this may not be the first time you have shared this story with someone. You may have shared a version of the story with the police or others just to get the details out there. When we ask you to share the story with supportive others, we mean think about sharing more of the details or even all of the details with at least one person. This sharing includes your emotional reactions, which you might not have shared with the police or in the "report version."

Similar to emotional processing from Chapter 3, keep talking about the experience until you don't need to talk about it anymore. Let people be there for you, just like you would want to be there for them. These social connections can be a powerful protective factor, help you feel less alone in your pain, and offer a different perspective on your difficult experience. Social connections can help you feel worthwhile at a time when you may not be feeling so good about yourself. Next, we will work on *how* to get started.

CHECK IN WITH YOURSELF

In the spaces below, list some people who you could potentially talk to about the difficult experience. Consider this *very* broadly as there are some people you might speak to who are not in your normal circle of family and friends but whom you trust and respect. This list can include people you don't usually talk to. For example, if the event happened at work, maybe list some coworkers who might understand or be able to offer perspective on what happened. If you are religious, perhaps there is a clergy person with whom you would want to share the story.

1. _____

2. _____

3. _____

4. _____

5. _____

Choose two people from the above list and, on the lines below, write down a plan to connect with them this week. This connection can be anything from a text or phone call to a walk around the block to sitting down for a deeper conversation. Just pick two people you can connect with this week at any level, and, on the lines below, specify what you want that connection to be. For example, "I'll call my sister Irina, and I will see if Lynne wants to walk around the block." We don't want you to feel isolated or alone. If you cannot think of a single person to try to connect with this week, try going someplace where people gather in a social setting, such as a neighborhood cafe or a sporting event. It is important to connect with and say things to another person, even if you don't know them and the connection does not need to be about the difficult experience.

1. _____

_____

2. _____

_____

Decide and then note on the above lines if you want these contacts to be focused on your difficult experience or a more general "touching base." Also note the date and time that you plan to initiate these social connections this week. It is helpful if you put these into your calendar or phone with a reminder. Try to allow at least 15 minutes for each connection, and try to make it a meaningful conversation. If you think the person would understand, you can let them know you're having a hard time with what happened. If they don't know about the difficult experience, that might be a place to start, even without a lot of details. For example, "I've been thinking a lot about a patient I lost to COVID." Or "My wife left me, and I'm really having a hard time with this divorce." Or "Do you remember that car wreck I had a few months ago? I'm still having a hard time with it."

After you complete each connection this week, complete Worksheet 5.1: Social Connections Weekly Process and Planning, located near the end of this chapter and in Appendix A at the end of this workbook, to consider how your connection went and what your plan is to continue to engage in social connections. For an example of how ICU nurse David completed his Social Connections Weekly Processing and Planning, look at Figure 5.1: David's Completed Social Connections Weekly Processing and Planning (Worksheet 5.1).

WORKSHEET 5.1: Social Connections Weekly Process and Planning

Social Connection 1   Week 1 Starting Date: <u>06/19/2020</u>

Who is one person you talked to this week? <u>Anna</u>

How many times did you connect this week? <u>twice</u>

How long was the longest conversation? <u>20 minutes</u>

Did you focus on: (DIFFICULT EXPERIENCE)   OTHER: _____

How did you feel after talking? **Rate yourself on the scale below:**

0---------1----------2---------3----------(4)----------5-----------6----------7----------8---------9----------10
Better   **Same**   **Worse**

Note anything important about the contact: <u>Anna listened and made me feel like my reactions are a normal part of when our patients die. She heard me and did not judge my thoughts and that helped me feel better and less guilty.</u>

After you have connected, consider how it went. Were you able to share your feelings? How did you feel afterward? What do you want to try differently next time? <u>Anna listened and I think it went as well as can be expected. I would do it the same next time.</u>

Would you want to repeat this social connection? If so, write down your plan for how to do that below. If not, plan an alternate social connection for next week. <u>I think it would feel weird to try and have this conversation again with Anna. I also feel kind of done with that piece of it.</u>

Social Connection 2   Week 1 Starting Date: <u>06/20/2020</u>

Who is one person you talked to this week? <u>Ron</u>

How many times did you connect this week? <u>Once</u>

How long was the longest conversation? <u>15 minutes</u>

Did you focus on: (DIFFICULT EXPERIENCE)   OTHER: _____

How did you feel after talking? Rate yourself on the scale below:

0---------1----------2---------3----------4----------(5)----------6----------7----------8----------9----------10
Better   **Same**   **Worse**

Note anything important about the contact: <u>Ron was a bit uncomfortable hearing about this work stress situation, but he listened as we watched the basketball game. He told me that he does not know how I do it with such a stressful job and the increase in patients with the pandemic. He said to let him know if I need to talk again and that was nice.</u>

After you have connected, consider how it went. Were you able to share your feelings? How did you feel afterward? What do you want to try differently next time? <u>I shared some feelings and I think it may help to talk with him again and share a bit more. He was listening but we were also watching the game and I think he was not fully attending to me. I really like Ron's perspective on things so talking more with him may be helpful.</u>

Would you want to repeat this social connection? If so, write down your plan for how to do that below. If not, plan an alternate social connection for next week. <u>I will do this one again with Ron next week when we already have a plan to meet for lunch.</u>

FIGURE 5.1 DAVID'S COMPLETED SOCIAL CONNECTIONS WEEKLY PROCESS AND PLANNING (WORKSHEET 5.1)

Tips for Social Support

1. Pick people who you believe can be supportive and not judgmental.
2. Talk to more than one person.
3. Consider how much of the story you want to share with each person.
4. Keep talking about your difficult experience until you don't need to talk about it anymore.
5. Spend time with people; it doesn't have to be about your messy memory.

Please complete a new Worksheet 5.1: Social Connections Weekly Process and Planning for each week that you are working on social connections. As you complete each week, think about adding different people to connect with the next week as opposed to the current week. The goals of social connection are (1) real connection and (2) building more connections so that you have a wider and more effective network of support. The more you reach out, the more people can be there for you, both with the difficult experience and for your life as you move on. Sharing with people on a deeper level is how we build intimacy and trust. It is how we forge friendships. Continue practicing this social connection skill until you feel that you have a few reliable social connections. Once you have these social connections, maintain them! You have to put in face time and talk time to keep these connections strong. Then, you can pull out this exercise in the future if you ever feel that you want to broaden or enhance your social network or to remind you to reach out.

WORKSHEET 5.1: Social Connections Weekly Process and Planning

Social Connections   Week 1 Starting Date: _____

Who is one person you talked to this week? _____

How many times did you connect this week? _____

How long was the longest conversation? _____

Did you focus on: DIFFICULT EXPERIENCE _____   OTHER: _____

How did you feel after talking? **Rate yourself on the scale below:**

0---------1---------2---------3----------4----------5----------6----------7----------8----------9----------10
Better   **Same**   **Worse**

Note anything important about the contact: _____

After you have connected, consider how it went. Were you able to share your feelings? How did you feel afterward? What do you want to try differently next time? _____

_____

Do you want to repeat this social connection? If so, write down your plan for how to do that below. If not, plan an alternate social connection for next week. _____

_____

Social Connections   Week 2 Starting Date: _____

Who is one person you talked to this week? _____

How many times did you connect this week? _____

How long was the longest conversation? _____

Did you focus on: DIFFICULT EXPERIENCE _____   OTHER: _____

How did you feel after talking? **Rate yourself on the scale below:**

0---------1---------2---------3----------4----------5----------6----------7----------8----------9----------10
Better   **Same**   **Worse**

Social Connections   Week 3 Starting Date: _____

Who is one person you talked to this week? _____

How many times did you connect this week? _____

How long was the longest conversation? _____

Did you focus on: DIFFICULT EXPERIENCE _____   OTHER: _____

How did you feel after talking? Rate yourself on the scale below:

0---------1---------2---------3----------4----------5----------6----------7----------8----------9----------10
Better   **Same**   **Worse**

Social Connections   Week 4 Starting Date: _____

Who is one person you talked to this week? _____

How many times did you connect this week? _____

How long was the longest conversation? _____

Did you focus on: DIFFICULT EXPERIENCE _____   OTHER: _____

How did you feel after talking? Rate yourself on the scale below:

0----------1----------2----------3----------4----------5----------6----------7----------8----------9----------10
Better   **Same**   **Worse**

Social Connections   Week 5 Starting Date: _____

Who is one person you talked to this week? _____

How many times did you connect this week? _____

How long was the longest conversation? _____

Did you focus on: DIFFICULT EXPERIENCE _____   OTHER: _____

How did you feel after talking? Rate yourself on the scale below:

0----------1----------2----------3----------4----------5----------6----------7----------8----------9----------10
Better   **Same**   **Worse**

Social Connections   Week 6 Starting Date: _____

Who is one person you talked to this week? _____

How many times did you connect this week? _____

How long was the longest conversation? _____

Did you focus on: DIFFICULT EXPERIENCE _____   OTHER: _____

How did you feel after talking? Rate yourself on the scale below:

0----------1----------2----------3----------4----------5----------6----------7----------8----------9----------10
Better   **Same**   **Worse**

CHAPTER 6

Self-Care

CATCHING UP WITH OUR CASE EXAMPLES

Ann

Once Ann started working on the memory of the sexual assault, she decided she needed to make other changes as well. Using the self-care strategies we will learn in this chapter, Ann started with reducing alcohol use and stopped smoking marijuana. It was hard at first, but she quickly saw benefits and had more energy. Next, Ann went back to her yoga studio and reconnected with her friends and her yoga instructor, Robin, while also getting the benefits of yoga practice. She had forgotten how good she felt after a class and how yoga helps build her resilience for the stress and hassles of daily life. Ann had not seen Robin since the rape, and they started to have lunch together. All of these ways of taking care of herself made Ann feel more in control of her life again, like she was doing the things she wanted to do instead of letting the rape force her to stay home.

David

David knew he wasn't taking care of himself, and it was affecting everything. When he decided to work on his self-care, David started by reducing his alcohol use and increasing his exercise. You can see his progress in Figure 6.1. (This figure is a combination of several worksheets from this chapter, all of which are located toward the end of this chapter and in Appendix A at the end of this workbook.) David's friend Angela was very supportive in helping him reach his goals, and he

Day	Week 1 goal: Only have 1 drink at a time after shift	Week 2 goal: Only have 1 drink at a time after shift every other day	Week 3 goal: Only have 1 drink at a time 3 days	Week 4 goal: Only drink socially	Week 5 goal: Practice 1 week abstinence	Week 6 goal: Only drink socially
Monday	✓	✓	✓	✓	✓	✓
Tuesday			✓	✓	✓	✓
Wednesday		✓	✓	✓	✓	✓
Thursday	✓		✓		✓	✓
Friday		✓		✓	✓	✓
Saturday			✓	✓	✓	✓
Sunday	✓	✓	✓	✓	✓	✓

Day	Week 1 goal: Walk Lucy after shift	Week 2 goal: Take Lucy on walks on days off	Week 3 goal: Walk more during shift	Week 4 goal: Walk 15 minutes during shift	Week 5 goal: Walk 30 minutes after shifts	Week 6 goal: Walk 30 minutes a day at work or after
Monday	✓	✓	✓	✓	✓	✓
Tuesday	✓		✓	✓	✓	✓
Wednesday	✓	✓	✓	✓		
Thursday	✓		✓		✓	✓
Friday	✓	✓		✓		✓
Saturday	✓		✓	✓	✓	✓
Sunday	✓		✓	✓	✓	✓

Day	Week 1 goal: No vending machine snacks	Week 2 goal: Take healthy snacks to work	Week 3 goal: Make dinner at least 3 nights	Week 4 goal: Take healthy snacks to work	Week 5 goal: Cut out unhealthy snacks after shift	Week 6 goal: Eat more healthy every day
Monday	✓	✓	✓	✓	✓	✓
Tuesday	✓	✓		✓	✓	✓
Wednesday	✓	✓	✓	✓		
Thursday		✓	✓	✓	✓	✓
Friday	✓	✓		✓		✓
Saturday	✓		✓	✓	✓	✓
Sunday	✓		✓	✓	✓	✓

FIGURE 6.1 DAVID'S COMPLETED ALCOHOL, HEALTHY EATING, AND EXERCISE SELF-MONITORING WORKSHEETS

decided to challenge himself to improve his eating habits as well. Specifically, he decided to stop getting vending machine snacks at work and instead brought fresh fruit and vegetables for snacks each day. After a month of changing his snack habits at work and at night, David had lost 5 pounds and had more energy for his day. Practicing self-care monitoring skills was helpful to keep him on target over the weeks.

Miguel

Miguel had already stopped drinking as part of his treatment for posttraumatic stress disorder (PTSD). When he got to the self-care work in the *Making Meaning of Difficult Experiences* program, he was ready to focus on sleep. Since his PTSD symptoms improved with prolonged exposure, he rarely had nightmares about the IED incident. However, he still had trouble falling asleep and often woke up at night. He focused on sleep hygiene and specifically reducing caffeine intake in the afternoon to help him fall asleep.

Shaquila

Shaquila had been eating very healthily intentionally when she was trying to get pregnant and continued healthy eating when she was pregnant. She didn't drink any alcohol and was exercising regularly. When she lost the baby, at first, she stayed in bed and didn't eat at all. Once she moved to the couch, she would eat mindlessly and drink wine all evening. She went to work and came home and vegged on the couch, and this was her life. Once she started working this program and started feeling better, she got more active as we discussed in Chapter 4. She knew she needed to take better care of herself, just like she was tending to her garden. By working in the garden when she came home from work, it kept her off the couch. She stopped the snacking in the evening, decreased drinking in the evenings and drank primarily while socializing, and started exercising again. At first, she and Tanja would walk around the neighborhood, and that helped her start exercising again. Shaquila started yoga again online and realized how much she had missed it. Soon she was riding her exercise bike again and back into a regular exercise routine. It was around this time she felt ready to go back to the doctor to see when she could try to get pregnant again.

What do you do—just for yourself—to take care of you? Some people exercise or pray or meditate for self-care. Others do crossword puzzles, play an instrument, take bubble baths, or listen to music or dance. Appendix B, "Suggestions for Pleasant Activities," near the end of this workbook, contains a long list of self-care activities that many people like to do. Please read through this list and check off the things that sound pleasant to you.

As noted in earlier chapters, sometimes when things are stressful, we don't take very good care of ourselves. Sometimes there is so much going on, it feels selfish to sleep enough or eat properly or take time to exercise or rest. You may notice that you don't do the things you love as often when you are under stress. It is easy to stop doing those activities during stress because they feel less important than the stressful event, but we know that taking care of ourselves and recharging through the activities we enjoy can make us better able to think, deal with stress, and be more productive.

This chapter on self-care will help you practice healthy habits including getting enough sleep, eating properly, exercising, and making sure you're doing fun things in life to keep being your best self. You will notice that some of this chapter overlaps with Chapter 4, "Getting Active" and with Chapter 5, "The Healing Power of Social Connection" and that's intentional. The most important point is to get you living your best life; it doesn't matter so much what you call it!

SELF-CARE ASSESSMENT

To begin, we would like you to assess different aspects of taking good care of yourself. As in all the other chapters of *Making Meaning of Difficult Experiences*, if you are already doing what you need to do and just need to continue that, you don't need to work on it here and can either skip through this section or move to the next chapter. That said, we do suggest you read through this material anyway to make sure you are not forgetting anything and perhaps to get some pointers.

Eating

Healthy eating is important for our health and well-being.

How healthy is your current diet? *Please put a mark on the line below*:

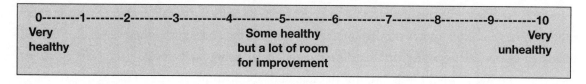

Sleeping

Getting sufficient restful sleep is important to function at our best.

Please answer the following on the blanks after each question:

How many hours of sleep do you typically get each night? _____ hours

How many hours do you need to feel rested? _____ hours

Desired sleep ratio: How many hours you get _____/How many hours you need _____

For example, if you need 8 hours to feel rested but usually get 6 hours, your desired sleep ratio is 6/8 or 75%.

Exercising

Physical exercise is important for our health and well-being to keep our bodies functioning at their best.

Please answer the following on the blanks after each question:

What kinds of exercises do you do regularly? Pick all that apply:

____Aerobic: examples include running, swimming, biking

____Strength: examples include weightlifting, push-ups

____Stretching: examples include yoga, Pilates

How often/per week? _____

How long per occasion? _____

Add for the total number of minutes per week: ____

Alcohol

Generally, we see no problem with drinking alcohol responsibly. However, consuming alcohol can be one of those "slippery slopes" following a stressful event.

Please answer the following on the blanks after each question:

How often do you drink per week? _____ times per week

How many drinks per occasion? _____

[Note: Current US guidelines say that more than 2 drinks per day (14 per week) for men and 1 drink per day (7 per week) for women is considered risky.]

Do you feel like you are drinking more than is good for you? _____ Yes _____ No

Do you drink specifically to forget your day or distract yourself from your feelings?

_____ Yes _____ No

Do you drink specifically to distract yourself from feelings or thoughts associated with this stressful event? _____ Yes _____ No

Does anyone close to you think you are drinking too much? _____ Yes _____ No

What to work on is *your* decision, but sometimes we should consider what people who love or care about us think.

Some habits can be very challenging to change on our own. Alcohol or drug use can be one of those habits, especially in the wake of difficult or traumatic experiences. The National Institute on Alcohol Abuse and Alcoholism has an excellent online resource called *Rethinking Drinking* that you can review to consider your use of alcohol and whether you may want to reduce or stop using alcohol (https://www.rethinkingdrinking.niaaa.nih.gov/). If you feel like you need help to reduce or stop using drugs or alcohol, treatment programs are available. Many people need a helping hand to make these changes, and asking for help takes strength. Please refer to Appendix C in this workbook for some resources that might help.

Drugs

Drugs refer to street drugs or prescription drugs used other than as prescribed. Like alcohol, drugs can be one of those "slippery slopes" following a stressful event.

Please answer the following on the blanks after each question:

How many days do you use drugs per week? _____ days per week _____times per day

Do you feel like you are using drugs more than is good for you? _____ Yes _____ No

Do you feel like you want to reduce your drug use? _____ Yes _____ No

Does anyone close to you think you are using drugs too much? _____ Yes _____ No

What to work on is *your* decision, but sometimes we should consider what people who love or care about us think.

As noted above, if you feel like you need help to reduce or stop using drugs or alcohol, treatment programs are available. Many people need a helping hand to make these changes, and asking for help takes strength. Please refer to Appendix C in this workbook for some resources that might help.

Enjoyable Activities

Enjoyable activities are healthy activities that bring you joy. (Do not include watching TV if you are just "vegging out.")

Please answer the following on the blanks after each question:

How often per week are you doing something you enjoy? _____ times per week

How long per occasion? _____ minutes/hours (circle one)

If you are having trouble coming up with fun things to do, take a look at the "Suggestions for Pleasant Activities" in Appendix B for some ideas of things people enjoy doing.

CREATING ACTION PLANS

Similar to the getting active plans you created in Chapter 4 and the social connections plans you created in Chapter 5, in this chapter we will create action plans to improve your self-care. Your action plans may progress from week to week, such as going to sleep 15 minutes earlier every night for a week, then 15 minutes earlier than that the next week, or you may repeat the same action plan from week to week, such as packing a healthy lunch to bring to work. If you feel you don't need any help in a particular area, feel free to skip it. These exercises are intended to help you in the way you would find useful.

Healthy Eating Habits

Part of taking care of ourselves is fueling our bodies with nutritious food. When we are stressed, however, it is easy to not take the time to make healthy choices, which can lead us to not functioning at our best. We need to make time to eat properly so we can feel our best.

OPT OUT: "I'm OK with my eating habits." Feel free to skip this exercise.

Otherwise, turn to Worksheet 6.1: Healthy Eating Habits, near the end of this chapter and also available in Appendix A near the end of this workbook.

Healthy Sleeping Habits

As mentioned before, we need to take care of ourselves before we can take care of others. Part of this self-care is "recharging" our bodies with sleep. When we are stressed, we often don't take the time to rest and sleep, the result of which is we don't function at our best. It is very important to develop healthy sleeping habits and take time for sleep. Aim for whatever you need to feel rested, which for most people is 6 to 8 hours per night. For many people, it can be difficult to sleep when they are under stress. Such people may have a hard time getting enough sleep each night, whereas others may find their bodies want to keep on sleeping or they might stay in bed to avoid the stress of a new day. Is your sleep impacted by stress? Are you sleeping more than usual? Less than usual? Are you feeling rested when you get up, or are you still tired?

> What you do before and during sleep is called *sleep hygiene*, and this can impact how restful and rejuvenated you feel when you wake up. Working on sleep hygiene can help you get the most out of your sleep time.

What Is Sleep Hygiene, and Why Is It Important?

"Sleep hygiene" refers to good sleep habits. Problems with sleep are common following stressful events, and this is normal. In fact, most people will have problems falling or staying asleep after experiencing a life-threatening event or while undergoing a difficult experience. What you do in response to sleep problems can have a significant impact on whether these problems are temporary and get better or if they continue over time.

Insomnia is an ongoing issue for some people. If you react to sleep problems with unhelpful thoughts such as, "I will never sleep well again" or "I have to get to sleep tonight, or I won't be able to function tomorrow," you are more likely to have worsening insomnia over time. In addition to unhelpful thoughts and insomnia, if you develop unhelpful sleep habits and poor sleep hygiene, you are more likely to experience continued sleep problems.

Stress disrupts sleep in many people, so good sleep hygiene is even more important when someone experiences a difficult event and has high levels of stress. The following suggestions for sleep hygiene can be helpful right after a difficult experience as well as for continued sleep problems:

- *Reduce stimulants late in the day, including caffeine and sugar.* Some people can keep on taking stimulants (like drinking caffeinated coffee or eating chocolate) until after dinner and that will not interfere with sleep, but for some people who are sensitive to caffeine, sugar, or chocolate, stopping at lunchtime may make it easier to fall asleep. If you find that you are having trouble falling asleep and you consume caffeine after lunch, stopping caffeine earlier in the day can be a good initial change to see if your sleep problems improve. Also keep in mind that, as we get older, our bodies may react to caffeine differently, and we may need to change when and how much caffeine we consume.
- *Avoid alcohol close to bedtime.* Even though it may make you feel drowsy, alcohol actually interferes with good sleep. With alcohol, the typical guide is to stop drinking about 2 hours before going to sleep.
- *Standardize life routines (sleep–wake, meals, exercise).* We suggest going to sleep and waking up at the same time every day, including weekends. When your body is used to a pattern of sleep and wake, it is more able to maintain the cycle when other things vary (such as life stress).
- *Avoid strenuous physical activity close to bedtime.* Exercise is great, but not too close to bedtime. Experts suggest stopping strenuous exercise at least an hour before going to sleep.
- *Never look at the clock when you are trying to sleep.* Turn the clock away from you to avoid looking at the time. Looking at the clock wakes you up more, which you do not want to do when you are trying to sleep. To see the time, you may have to physically change positions and raise your head, and then light comes into your eyes from the numbers on the clock display at a time when it is supposed to be dark. You may then have thoughts about what time it is, and your body can react to those thoughts and wake you up even more. There is never a good time for it to be when you are trying to sleep and are not asleep. If it is early in the night when you look at the clock, this might cause you stress worrying it will be a bad night. If it is early in the morning, it might cause you stress worrying that you won't get back to sleep and will be tired the next day. It is important to remember that, from time to time, we all experience less than restful sleep, and we do actually function fine the next day. It is not a catastrophe.

- *Go to bed when sleepy.* Even if it is bedtime, don't lie down until you feel like you will sleep soon after your head hits the pillow. Being tired and sleepy are not the same thing. You can be tired and wired! Learn to recognize when you are sleepy. When you are sleepy, don't keep doing something else; stop that activity and go to sleep.

- *Use the bed only for sleep (and sex).* We don't want the bed associated with not sleeping, so only get in bed to sleep or have sex. It is not a spot in which to routinely read or watch television.

- *Get out of bed if you're not sleeping and only return when sleepy.* If you are not asleep in the amount of time you would usually fall asleep, get out of bed and do something else. Do not do something activating or stimulating—do something boring. Do not get on the computer or use any screen.

- *Do not use electronics or screens 1 hour before bed.* Research has shown that looking at computer, tablet, or phone screens close to bedtime interferes with sleep. No video games within 1 hour of bedtime!

- *Set an alarm and wake up at the same time every day.* Set the alarm for the time you really need to wake up. Then when it goes off, get out of bed. **Do not hit the snooze button.** Hitting the snooze button may feel luxurious, but it is not good-quality sleep and therefore is wasting time. Some people tell us they feel more groggy after hitting the snooze button.

- *Avoid naps.* If you are having problems sleeping at night, we suggest you avoid naps or *siestas*. If you nap, you won't be ready to go to sleep when it is time, which means you might feel tired the next day, and this can become a vicious cycle.

Tips for Sleep Hygiene

1. Reduce stimulants (like caffeine) late in day or even after lunch.
2. Avoid alcohol close to bedtime.
3. Standardize life routines:

   Go to sleep and wake up at the same time every day.

   Eat meals at the same time every day.

   Exercise at similar times on days you exercise.
4. Avoid strenuous exercise within an hour of bedtime.
5. Go to bed only when sleepy.
6. Use your bed only for sleep (and sex). You do not want to associate the bed with the anxiety of not falling asleep.
7. Once you are in bed, never look at the clock.
8. If you are having trouble falling asleep and have been in bed for what feels like a while, get up and do something boring or relaxing out of bed and then return when you feel drowsy.
9. Set your alarm and wake at the same time each day. DO NOT use your snooze button as snoozing is not restorative sleep.

OPT OUT: "I'm OK with my sleeping habits." Feel free to skip this exercise.

Otherwise, turn to Worksheet 6.2: Healthy Sleeping Habits, near the end of this chapter and also available in Appendix A near the end of this workbook.

Healthy Exercise Habits

Part of taking care of yourself is keeping your body and mind healthy through exercise. When we are stressed, it is easy to not exercise and then we are not functioning at our best. You can choose the kind of activity you want to do as long as you are getting out and moving around. Try to make this fun by listening to music, walking outside, walking with a friend, or varying activities. It can be helpful to put your exercise times on your phone or calendar.

Exercise, especially regular aerobic exercise, is as effective at reducing mild depression as is antidepressant medication. Exercise is not a treatment for PTSD or depression, but it does help in managing stress, building stamina, maintaining physical health, and usually improving mood. The most recent federal guidelines (from 2018) suggest that adults should do at least 150 minutes up to 300 minutes a week of moderate-intensity, or 75 minutes up to 150 minutes a week of vigorous-intensity aerobic physical activity or an equivalent combination of moderate- and vigorous-intensity aerobic activity. In addition, muscle-strengthening activities on 2 or more days a week is also recommended. Exercising outside has the double benefit of exercise and the refreshing effect of being in nature. Find an exercise that you can do regularly and relatively easily so that you can start a new positive habit that will continue over time. Something that you can do for low cost and at home has the best likelihood of becoming a healthy and consistent habit.

Be creative in how you think about exercise and consider changing your routine from time to time. Trying new types of exercise can help keep your body and mind flexible. Whether you decide to run, do yoga, engage in Pilates, or dance, all can be wonderful ways to keep your body moving and your brain active.

Tips for Exercising

1. The Department of Health and Human Services recommends at least 150 minutes of moderate aerobic activity or 75 minutes of vigorous aerobic activity a week, or a combination of moderate and vigorous activity.
2. Choose an activity that gets you out of the house and moving.
3. Make it fun—listen to music, walk outside, bring a friend, change it up.
4. Put your exercise times on your calendar or phone.

OPT OUT: "I'm OK with my exercise habits." Feel free to skip this exercise.

Otherwise, turn to Worksheet 6.3: Healthy Exercise Habits, near the end of this chapter and also available in Appendix A near the end of this workbook.

Alcohol and Drug Use

As noted several times before, we need to take care of ourselves before we can take care of others. Part of self-care is either not using recreational alcohol and drugs or using them in moderation if you choose to use. When we are stressed, it is easy to self-medicate with alcohol or drugs and then we are not functioning at our best. The guidelines for alcohol consumption recommend limiting consumption to 2 drinks per day (14 per week) for men and 1 drink per day (7 per week) for women. Recent research has shown a large increase in alcohol and drug use during the pandemic as more people have been at home and are dealing with many social and financial stressors and difficult experiences. Many people who never had issues with alcohol or drugs in the past are now struggling with problematic patterns of use and addiction. The consequences of use can be devastating including family conflict, health problems, employment issues, and even legal problems.

In the United States, one "standard" drink (or one alcoholic drink equivalent) contains roughly 14 grams of pure alcohol, which is found in

- 12 ounces of regular beer, which is usually about 5% alcohol.
- 5 ounces of wine, which is typically about 12% alcohol.
- 1.5 ounces of distilled spirits, which is about 40% alcohol.

Tips for Alcohol Consumption

If you drink alcoholic beverages, limit alcohol consumption to:

- 2 drinks per day (14 per week) for men, or
- 1 drink per day (7 per week) for women.

The recommendations differ for men and women based on differences in how alcohol is metabolized.

Consider how many standard drinks you consume in an average week. Has this changed recently or after a difficult experience? Is it impacting your health, social, or work function?

What about drug use? Are you using prescription medications (such as for pain or anxiety) more than prescribed? Are you using recreational drugs to self-medicate? Have you noticed your drug use increasing during times of stress or following the stressful event? Is anyone who cares about you worried about your alcohol or drug use?

OPT OUT: "I'm OK with my alcohol and drugs consumption." Feel free to skip this exercise.

Otherwise, turn to Worksheet 6.4: Alcohol/Drugs and Self-Care, near the end of this chapter and also available in Appendix A near the end of this workbook.

SELF-CARE AND YOU

Whatever we call it, self-care is at the heart of all that we do. When we care for ourselves, we are better able to accomplish our goals and care for others. Think about what you want to continue working on for your self-care goals, and keep in mind that this may change over the weeks, months, and years ahead. It can be helpful to revisit this chapter from time to time to consider whether you want to work on any of these key areas for self-care. We are all works in progress, and what we need to work on will change over time. Be kind to yourself and strive to be your best self each day.

We will review the skills and exercises presented in this workbook in Chapter 7 and discuss if and when to see a professional. Good for you for getting to this point!

WORKSHEET 6.1: Healthy Eating Habits

Set a goal for yourself that is easy to achieve right away and do every day, such as reducing snacks, eating 1 serving of a vegetable or fresh fruit, cutting down on soda or caffeine, or making your lunch for work, and commit to this goal starting immediately. For some people, stress leads to eating more while others find that stress reduces their appetite. Consider how stress is impacting your eating habits and set a manageable goal for yourself. You can work through your goal using the worksheets in this workbook, and you can modify your goals from week to week.

Healthy Eating Goal for This Week: Please write your healthy eating goals on the lines below.

_____

_____

Sometimes it can help to have a partner working on healthy eating habits with you. This person can be an ally to talk with about the challenges of changing your eating, and you can give each other tips for how to succeed. If it is someone you live with, that's even better, as you can work together on healthy meals and having healthy snacks in your place.

Who could help you with your healthy eating habits this week? _____

ACTION PLAN FOR HEALTHY EATING NEXT WEEK

After you have worked on your eating habits for 1 week, think about how it went. How did you feel afterward?

_____

What do you want to try differently next week? _____

ACTION ASSESSMENT

Do you want to work on your eating habits again next week? Do you want to keep the same goals or try something different? _____

_____

ASSESSMENT

On the table below, write your weekly goal, check off the days that you completed your healthy eating habits goal, and write in any comments.

Day	Week 1 goal: _____	Week 2 goal: _____	Week 3 goal: _____	Week 4 goal: _____	Week 5 goal: _____	Week 6 goal: _____
Monday						
Tuesday						
Wednesday						
Thursday						
Friday						
Saturday						
Sunday						

WORKSHEET 6.2: Healthy Sleeping Habits

The aim of this exercise is getting enough sleep to feel rested. For most people that is 6 to 8 hours per night. Set a goal for yourself that is easy to achieve right away and every day, such as getting up when your alarm goes off rather than hitting the snooze button or going to sleep 15 minutes earlier each night, and commit to your goal starting immediately. You can work through your goal using the worksheets in this workbook. Please evaluate how your healthy sleeping action plan is going each week. Feel free to keep the same goals from week to week or change them.

Healthy Sleeping Goal for This Week:

_____

ACTION PLAN FOR HEALTHY SLEEPING NEXT WEEK

After you have worked on your sleep habits for 1 week, think about how it went. How did you feel afterward?

_____

What do you want to try differently next week? _____

ACTION ASSESSMENT

Do you want to work on your sleeping habits next week? Do you want to keep the same goals or try something different? _____

ASSESSMENT

On the table below, write your weekly goal, check off the days that you completed your healthy sleeping habits goal, and write in any comments.

Day	Week 1 goal: _____	Week 2 goal: _____	Week 3 goal: _____	Week 4 goal: _____	Week 5 goal: _____	Week 6 goal: _____
Monday						
Tuesday						
Wednesday						
Thursday						
Friday						
Saturday						
Sunday						

WORKSHEET 6.3: Healthy Exercise Habits

Set a goal for yourself that is easy to achieve right away and regularly, such as 10 minutes a day walking on your treadmill or riding on your exercise bike, and commit to starting it immediately. If you do not have exercise equipment, use what you do have access to, such as taking a walk outside or doing an online yoga class. You can work through your goal using the worksheets in this workbook. After a week of working on healthy exercise habits, evaluate how it went with the questions below. It is fine to keep the same goals from week to week or to modify them. If you are building up a new exercise habit, you may want to gradually increase the amount of time you exercise until you hit your target and then you can aim for that each time.

Healthy Exercise Goal for This Week:

_____

Sometimes it can help to invite a friend to exercise with you, especially if you exercise together. This person can be an ally to talk with about the challenges of starting a new exercise plan. You can even provide support and give each other tips for how to succeed.

Who would you like to invite to help with your exercise goal? _____

ACTION PLAN FOR HEALTHY EXERCISING NEXT WEEK

After you have worked on your exercise habits for one week, think about how it went. How did you feel afterward? _____

What do you want to try differently next week? _____

ACTION ASSESSMENT

Do you want to work on your exercise habits next week? Do you want to keep the same goals or try something different? _____

ASSESSMENT

On the table below, write your weekly goal, check off the days that you completed your healthy exercise habits goal, and write in any comments.

Day	Week 1 goal: _____	Week 2 goal: _____	Week 3 goal: _____	Week 4 goal: _____	Week 5 goal: _____	Week 6 goal: _____
Monday						
Tuesday						
Wednesday						
Thursday						
Friday						
Saturday						
Sunday						

WORKSHEET 6.4: Alcohol/Drugs and Self-Care

Set a goal for yourself that is easy to achieve right away and every day, such as limiting your alcohol to 1 drink per day or smoking pot only 3 days per week. After a week of working on this goal, evaluate how it went with the questions below. Feel free to keep the same goals from week to week or modify them.

Alcohol/Drug Goal for This Week:

_____

If you choose to drink alcohol or use drugs:

1. Use recreational alcohol and drugs in moderation.
2. Don't self-medicate with alcohol or drugs when you are stressed.
3. Don't self-medicate with drugs or alcohol to deal with the feelings you get when you think about difficult experiences.

ACTION PLAN FOR ALCOHOL/DRUGS AND SELF-CARE NEXT WEEK

After you worked on your use of alcohol and/or substances for a week, how did it go? How did you feel afterward? _____

What do you want to try differently next week? _____

ACTION ASSESSMENT

Do you want to work on your alcohol and/or drug use next week? Do you want to keep the same goals or try something different? _____

ASSESSMENT

On the table below, write your weekly goal, check off the days you hit your target for reducing alcohol and drug use, and write in any comments.

Day	Week 1 goal: _____	Week 2 goal: _____	Week 3 goal: _____	Week 4 goal: _____	Week 5 goal: _____	Week 6 goal: _____
Monday						
Tuesday						
Wednesday						
Thursday						
Friday						
Saturday						
Sunday						

CHAPTER 7

Closing the Book on Difficult Experiences

CATCHING UP WITH OUR CASE EXAMPLES

Ann

We're hoping it is obvious by now how the different skills presented in the different chapters work together and overlap. By working on her memory and processing it following the assault, it helped Ann feel less guilty about the assault (she had initially felt responsible for her attack because she went to a club on her own) and made it a little easier for her to confide in her friends Samantha and Robin. By limiting her alcohol and drug intake, Ann was able to engage emotionally with the assault memory, which allowed the strong emotions to ease to a more manageable level. Ann decided to get more active; this decision opened up her world, which had become very narrow following the assault. This decision and processing work brought her back to yoga, which helped her physically and also brought her old friend Robin back into her life as an important social connection. Working on the activity of going grocery shopping after work helped Ann be more active and helped with her healthy eating goals. Just as our world can become narrower one decision at a time after a stressful experience, so it can start opening back up one decision at a time. The law of inertia states: objects at rest tend to stay at rest; objects in motion tend to stay in motion. By approaching the memory and reminders, Ann made her world bigger and better again.

Ann was able to make decisions that (1) helped her deal with the memory of the assault and not feel so guilty, (2) allowed her to open up to friends and therefore get their social support, and (3) got her more active and back to old activities and healthy habits such as practicing yoga and eating healthier. The assault in the bathroom stall at the club will always be something that should never have happened to her, but she was able to get her life back on track and felt stronger, healthier, and happier for the work that she accomplished.

David

After 2 weeks of working on the difficult experience and exploring the emotions, David had a very different perspective on the memory of his patient Clem's death. He moved from a place where he felt angry at other people (especially those who would not mask) and helpless, to still having some anger while also seeing that what he did at the time was helpful to Clem and provided comfort to this patient as he died. Approaching this difficult experience by using the worksheets in Chapter 3 of this workbook helped David to feel the emotions, stay with those emotions until they became less intense, and consider the whole situation in a new light. He realized that some of what made this situation with Clem so difficult was feeling helpless when his own father died from cancer, and these worksheets helped David understand the emotions related to his father's death and those that related to what happened with Clem. For David, this experience was no longer stuck.

In addition to working on his experience using the worksheets, David told Angela about working on the difficult experience. Angela was also involved in Clem's care and had been aware that David was struggling with burnout. Angela now notices that, as of this week, David seems to be bouncing back to his old self and is engaging with his patients and smiling more as he goes through his day. While David did not ask Angela to read the story he wrote about his difficult experience, they discussed some of his thoughts about the memory—like how being there can comfort people as they die—and Angela said she saw Clem relax when David came into the room that night. By approaching and feeling the emotions, David was able to move on from the difficult experience.

David also worked hard on getting active and reconnecting with friends and acquaintances, jump-started by dog-sitting and taking the dog for walks after work and on days off. These changes helped buoy him for the challenges of his work and made him feel human again. When he tried to shut down his emotions about Clem's death, he shut down all emotions. By processing those difficult emotions, David opened himself up to feeling emotions again, which helped him engage better with others and feel genuine and authentic. Eating better, drinking less alcohol, and exercising regularly again rounded out David's progress and gave him a sense of health and resilience in place of feeling like he was at the end of his rope. David was happy that *Making Meaning of Difficult Experiences* helped him take his life back from the death of Clem and he also knew that these skills could be used when he was confronted with other potentially traumatic events in his life moving forward.

Helen

Two years after the car accident Helen rarely thought about it. She was busy with work and taking care of her growing family, and she felt fully able to drive and engage with her life. She was very happy to have had the opportunity to work with the team in the ER on the memory of the accident, and she attributes this work to her current full recovery.

Miguel

Miguel worked hard in treatment for his posttraumatic stress disorder (PTSD). After completing prolonged exposure (PE) therapy, he no longer met the criteria for a diagnosis of PTSD, and he had 6 months of abstinence from alcohol under his belt. Even with this success, he still had some areas he wanted to work on. Specifically, Miguel wanted to reconnect with his family and military social network and improve his sleep. *Making Meaning of Difficult Experiences* offered skills that were familiar to him from PE and provided a framework that worked well for him. He maintained his gains in PTSD and alcohol use and reconnected with his family and two of his closest Army buddies. Finally, he was able to greatly improve his sleep through focusing on sleep hygiene. Miguel felt like a different person and was happy again.

Shaquila

Shaquila worked through her miscarriage using all of the exercises in this workbook. After just a couple weeks she felt like a dark cloud was lifted off of her brain. She woke up feeling happy and ready to start her day. She started to feel optimistic about trying another course of IVF. Tanja was happy to see her partner back to herself again and they scheduled with the doctor to try again to start their family.

We hope that *Making Meaning of Difficult Experiences* and, if you used it, the Messy Memories app have been helpful. We hope these can be resources for you to use now and in the future if you go through other difficult experiences. The unfortunate truth is that most of us will encounter a difficult or even traumatic experience in our lifetimes, but the good news is that most of us will be able to process it and get back on track.

REVIEW OF THE SKILLS IN *MAKING MEANING OF DIFFICULT EXPERIENCES*

Chapter 1, "Traumatic Experiences," described difficult experiences and discussed how people can get stuck in stressful and potentially traumatic experiences leading to anxiety, guilt, and depression. We focused on how difficult and potentially traumatic experiences are common and what makes certain experiences more likely to "get stuck." We then moved on to provide an overview of the program and how you can work through these experiences using the skills in this workbook.

Remember the concept of posttraumatic growth from Chapter 2, "Why Approach Difficult Experiences"? Posttraumatic growth refers to a sense of positive change following exposure to traumatic experiences. More specifically, following difficult and potentially traumatic experiences, many people feel a sense of accomplishment in survival and a new purpose or focus in life. For many, a sense of gratitude for survival and a desire to give back to ensure that their survival has meaning is important and can take the shape of closer family relationships or public service or a new vocation.

> Going through tough times often gives us appreciation for what matters most to us. It helps build strength and confidence in ourselves that we can withstand tough experiences and even grow from them. We feel stronger and develop the knowledge that if and when tough things happen in the future, we will be able to handle them.

Posttraumatic growth is one type of "resilience response," and there is no resilience without adversity. *Resilience* refers to coming through tough times strengthened in coping or other resources such that the next tough experience is less damaging. Resilience is by far the most common outcome for survivors. We hope this workbook can help even more people move through the storms of life and emerge on the other side stronger and more resilient. We hope the memory processing and skills emphasized in this workbook encourage both resilience and posttraumatic growth.

At this point we hope that you have been using the program to address at least one difficult experience. As you recall, we can address these difficult experiences through approaching the memory—not avoiding it—and letting ourselves feel the emotions associated with the memory. Chapter 3, "Memory Exposure and Processing," provides a framework for you to approach the memory of a difficult experience. Using the Worksheet 3.1: Mood Thermometers, you checked in with yourself each week to see how you were feeling. This can be useful as a quick way to get your bearings when you are dealing with stress and difficult experiences. After checking in, you started digging into the difficult experience by choosing a difficult experience that felt "stuck" or caused you to feel distressed or overwhelmed. You decided what you wanted to work on and where the memory started and ended. Then you used Worksheet 3.2: Difficult Experience Writing Exercise and Worksheet 3.3: Difficult Experience Processing Exercise—and possibly the Messy Memories app—to revisit the memory of the difficult experience while allowing yourself to feel the emotions connected to the experience.

We hope that using these worksheets and thinking about and answering the questions helped you come to a new understanding of the difficult experience you chose to address. The process may not have been easy, but with time and focused work on approaching instead of avoiding, memories of difficult experiences *can* get easier. You may have seen changes occur when you remembered details you had not thought about or when approaching the memory got easier through constant revisiting of the difficult experience's memory. These changes in how you see the difficult experience likely led to changes in how you see the experience. Alternatively, these changes may have led you to change how you think about yourself. For example, did you find yourself feeling stronger? Less afraid of the memory? Did you find yourself feeling more confident or more able to handle bumps in the road of life? As you learned that you can feel very strong negative emotions while approaching the difficult experience memory in this program, we hope that you also experienced that these feelings are not as difficult to experience as they once were and may eventually go away if you stick with it and do not avoid.

Furthermore, you experienced that, even when the writing exercise and/or reviewing exercise are hard to do, nothing permanently bad happens to you. You are strong and resilient. You survived the difficult experience in the best way that you could. Worksheets 3.5 to 3.8 then gave you a framework to dig deep into your emotional experience at the time of the difficult experience, and now as you revisit the difficult experience, you can think about the situation differently in a way that doesn't haunt you. We hope that the skills led you to a new understanding of who you are as a person and how you can overcome life's struggles.

As we said at the start of this workbook, these changes require you to do the work. Most people will need to spend about 6 to 8 weeks of focused work to see the difficult experience truly fall back into the rearview mirror of your life, but you should feel free to use this workbook in any way that works best for you.

While Chapter 3, "Memory Exposure and Processing," is the heart of this difficult experience work, the program also encourages additional healthy skills. Chapter 4, "Getting Active," looks at the low motivation that can easily set in when you are confronted with stressful and difficult experiences. It is common following a difficult experience to have trouble getting outside of your head, and you may have stopped doing things that you enjoy. Sometimes this comes out of being busy just keeping your head above water, trying to handle what you need in life. For some people, their lives get narrower if they avoid reminders of the stressful event and lose confidence in themselves or get depressed. Chapter 4 provides specific guidance using Worksheet 4.1: Your List of Daily Activities so you can look at your life and decide whether you need or want to add in more positive activities. Worksheet 4.2: Your Action Plan helps you set specific goals to make sure you are connecting with activities you enjoy. Ensuring that you work hard *and* still have time to do things that make you happy can be tough, but these activities recharge your emotional resources so that you can ride the waves of life successfully.

As you learned in Chapter 5, "The Healing Power of Social Connection," human beings are social animals, and we all need to feel connected to other people. However, many of us isolate following stressful experiences, especially if we feel guilty about them. Our social connections can help us in times of trouble and make us feel a part of the world and combat isolation. These connections help us feel not so alone in our pain and can offer support and perspectives that help us heal. Worksheet 5.1: Social Connections Weekly Process and Planning allows you to commit to a plan each week for how you would intentionally make social connections with existing friends and family or make new social connections. We hope that making a plan and committing to that plan helps you fit this skill into your busy day and increases how often you make these important social connections each week. Making these connections while you are working on a difficult experience is especially important as it gives you another person to talk to, which provides the chance to see new perspectives through their eyes and process the memory even more quickly than working on it alone.

Finally, Chapter 6, "Self-Care," encourages you to look at how you are taking care of yourself. If you do not care for yourself, you may not have the energy and drive to overcome tough times. It is not selfish to take care of yourself! We need to take care of ourselves to be able to help others. Worksheets 6.1 through 6.4 encourage a brief assessment of each area of self-care and then provide a chance for you to set a goal to commit to change in that area. The key areas of focus included healthy eating, healthy sleeping, healthy exercise, and moderation in alcohol and/or drug use. These are tools you can revisit any time in the future if you decide you want to address change in these areas of self-care.

> When you are in the middle of an emotional storm, it is hard to see that there may be a different way: *asking for help is often the most difficult step to take toward recovery*. Many of us do not recognize that we are having trouble with our emotions until something significant happens, like a fight, loss of a job, or some other consequence. Often, after treatment, people will say things like, "Wow! How could I not have seen what I was doing earlier?" or "Why did that seem normal at the time?" or "I wish I had done this sooner."

Approaching your difficult experiences through *Making Meaning of Difficult Experiences* can be an initial step toward the other side of those experiences. Now that you have completed the workbook and, if you used it, the Messy Memories app, we hope it has been helpful. Congratulations on completing this program! For many, this can take you through the experience and out the other side and be enough to get to where you want to be. For others, this may be a start to recognizing that professional help is needed to get all the way through your difficult experience. The next part of this chapter covers a bit about how to access additional resources, and Appendix C provides resources as well. Whatever you choose, you have taken the first steps by reading *Making Meaning of Difficult Experiences* and starting to work through this. *Congratulations on your resilience, and we wish you good luck!* We hope your road is an easy one, but if you encounter difficult experiences again, we hope you can turn to this book and app for the resources to help you through it.

KNOW WHEN TO ASK FOR HELP

Making Meaning of Difficult Experiences provides a framework to address tough, stressful, or even traumatic situations. Learning the skills presented in this workbook, connecting with people who can help support us, and practicing positive coping strategies can often help us to work through difficult experiences and move on with our lives. So even though we (Dr. Rauch and Dr. Rothbaum) encourage you to approach rather than avoid your difficult experiences and the emotions they trigger, it is important to know that mental health resources are available if you would like to use them or if you find that your reactions to the difficult experience are staying stuck or even getting worse as you work on them. Not everyone can do this work on their own, and that's OK. The following resources are varied and may include short- or longer-term programs and depend on your resources and what is available to you. For example, you may benefit from something short-term such as connecting with your primary care doctor or nurse practitioner to get medication to help with short-term sleep problems, or you may decide to connect with a psychologist or social worker. Psychotherapy may involve a treatment program using an evidence-based psychotherapy option, such as prolonged exposure for PTSD (typically 9 to 15 weekly sessions) or cognitive behavioral therapy (CBT) for anxiety or depression. For those in crisis, even more in-depth options include residential treatment, hospitalization, or substance use detoxification.

If you are not functioning as you need or want to in any area of your life—at work, socially, at home, physically—then your problem may be more serious than a self-help workbook can address, and you may require additional help. You may have a problem that could be diagnosed as PTSD, depression, or an anxiety disorder. If you are a worrier and you worry excessively about a number of different things, you may have generalized anxiety disorder. If, rather than processing the memory of your difficult experience, you are thinking about it over and over or "spinning your wheels" and can't move through the process to be able to think about it differently, you may require more help. If you are so paralyzed by fear, distress, guilt, or sadness that you have a hard time even thinking about your difficult experience or sticking with it, you may require a professional to help you process it. As we discussed in Chapter 6, "Self-Care," some habits can be very challenging to change on our own. Alcohol or drug use can be one of those difficult habits, especially in the wake of difficult or traumatic experiences. If you feel like you need help to reduce or stop using drugs or alcohol, treatment programs are available. Many people need a helping hand to make these changes, and asking for help takes strength.

Again, there is no shame in needing a higher level of help. You would want someone you care about to ask for help if they need it, right? Luckily, we have many treatments that work, and there are many professionals and agencies here to help. The most important thing is getting that help to get your life back on track. We know it takes courage to ask for help, but it is worth it. Resilience means going through difficult experiences and coming out of them with growth and recovery. There are lots of ways to be resilient; many people may be resilient and still have some trouble that they can use help to overcome. There is no resilience without adversity, and there are different kinds of resilience. One form is asking for help when it is needed. Be resilient!

Below we offer many suggestions. We present a number of PTSD-specific suggestions, but many of these organizations are resources for other mental health problems as well. We discuss different forms of treatment and what evidence-based care means in much more detail in our book, *PTSD: What Everyone Needs to Know*.

How to Find a Provider

If you haven't been able to achieve what you wanted to accomplish with *Making Meaning of Difficult Experiences*, there are several different resources for finding a provider. If you have insurance and want to use an in-network provider, go to your insurance website and search for mental health providers. Usually they have specialties listed. We recommend you contact them and ask what evidence-based treatments they provide for PTSD, depression, anxiety disorder, substance use disorders, and so on.

> If at any point you are having thoughts about harming yourself or someone else, you need to reach out to those around you and seek professional assistance immediately. Call 911 or go to your nearest emergency room or contact the National Suicide Prevention Lifeline at 988. This will take you to a person who can talk with you 24/7 about how you are feeling and work with you to figure out what help you need and how to access it.

For more information on related mental health treatments, look at our book, *PTSD: What Everyone Needs to Know*, where we review the many responses that people who have been through trauma and other difficult experiences may have, such as PTSD, depression, and alcohol and/or substance use disorders. In that book, we also discuss many possible treatment options to consider so that you can talk with your mental health provider about what might work best for you. Some of the material presented later in this chapter is taken from *PTSD: What Everyone Needs to Know*, although feel free to look at that book for a more in-depth discussion. Appendix C, "Additional Resources," near the end this workbook contains many resources that you may also find helpful.

What Kinds of Mental Health Providers Work with People After Difficult Experiences? How Do I Know if They Are Good?

In general, mental health treatments, including those for PTSD, can be divided into psychotherapy and medication. *Psychotherapy*, sometimes known as "talk therapy," is usually done one on one, with a therapist and the person seeking assistance. There are some treatments that are provided in groups. Therapists must be providers licensed by the state in which they practice or working through an interstate practice agreement, such as PsyPact, that allows psychologists to practice in states that accept the practice compact. Some of the most common types of mental health providers include the following:

- *Psychologists* typically have a PhD in clinical psychology but may have a PsyD and are not licensed to prescribe medication in most states.
- In most states, *social workers* can also be licensed to deliver therapy. Social workers typically have a master's degree in social work (e.g., MSW).
- *Psychiatrists* are medical doctors (MDs). They may prescribe medications and may also provide therapy.
- In some states, *nurse practitioners, physician assistants (PAs)*, and *clinical nurse specialists* (CNSs) may also prescribe medications supervised by a physician.

Check online at your Secretary of State website and make sure your provider is licensed. It is fine to ask a prospective provider questions about their experience and the kinds of treatments they use. Most people want to find a provider covered by their insurance plan, but it is even more important to find a provider who is experienced with effective treatments for the issues that you are experiencing, such as depression or PTSD. Most of the effective treatments that we describe for depression or PTSD do not require that many sessions, so even if the best provider is out of network, it may be a good short-term investment for long-term gain if you are able to afford it. If you have insurance, in most states, you can submit for reimbursement even if your provider is not listed on your plan. Many universities with psychology graduate programs or psychiatry residency programs offer low-cost clinics.

What Kinds of Therapies Help?

The types of therapy that have been shown to be helpful for most mental health issues are forms of Cognitive Behavioral Therapy (CBT). A CBT program

- tends to be very problem-focused (rather than focusing on the unconscious),
- is usually short-term (weeks rather than months),
- commonly has a skills-based focus (the therapist teaches skills in session), and
- usually involves assigning homework to practice the skills taught in the session.

CBT is very effective at treating problems involving anxiety and depression. For most anxiety and depressive problems, CBT would be recommended before trying medication if the person is new to treatment. Similar to doing exercise, once people learn the CBT skills in therapy, they need to continue practicing these skills even after therapy ends. When people continue to practice the skills, there is very little relapse. If a new difficult experience occurs, like the loss of a relationship or job or loved one, sometimes problems can increase. However, if the person continues to practice the skills that worked, such increases tend to be temporary.

CBT can include exercises aimed at thoughts, feelings, and behavior. One of the most effective techniques for troublesome thoughts is called *cognitive restructuring*. In cognitive restructuring, thoughts are examined to make sure they are rational, helpful, and based on facts. Common cognitive errors, such as jumping to conclusions, are identified and challenged, and the person is taught how to think more realistically and helpfully. Relaxation is often taught in CBT to help with tension and to help get to sleep. Techniques aimed at one's behavior help the person react more helpfully. For example, role-playing may be useful to practice how to have difficult conversations or give feedback. Exposure techniques may be useful if the person is avoiding realistically safe situations or reminders. If the person is doing compulsive behaviors—such as checking locks or handwashing—they may benefit from response prevention. In general, CBT is very specific to the problems the person is having.

For PTSD, trauma-focused therapies have been shown to be consistently effective and include prolonged exposure (PE) and other types of exposure therapy, cognitive therapy, cognitive processing therapy (CPT), and eye movement desensitization and reprocessing (EMDR). CBT for depression and alcohol and substance misuse are also highly effective and relatively short-term therapies.

Sometimes reaching out for help involves family or couples counseling. The types of providers listed above may provide family or couples counseling, although they require additional specific training. If you are looking for these services, ask your provider about their training in couples and/or family therapy. Family or couples treatments can be supportive and nonspecific or more focused on a specific issue or mental health problem, such as PTSD. Talk with your provider about what you want and what fits with your financial and time resources.

Seeking help may include getting involved with support groups or social groups at your house of worship or community center. Groups like Alcoholics Anonymous (AA) or Narcotics Anonymous (NA) provide support for those who want to stop using alcohol and other drugs, while Al-Anon and Nar-Anon provide support for family of those with alcohol or substance use disorders. The National Alliance on Mental Illness (NAMI) has many social support groups for family members of those suffering with mental health issues. They also can provide referrals for care and additional resources. Sometimes just getting out and connecting with people in any positive social setting can help you feel able to manage your life and difficult experiences. Joining the adult baseball team at your local YMCA or agreeing to help with the school picnic can sometimes provide the social contact that you need to feel connected to the world in a positive way.

There are other people whom you may find helpful to talk to about difficulties you are having. For example, you may want to consider talking with your clergy about what's going on. If you are working, you can reach out to your Employee Assistance Program (EAP). EAP personnel are usually required to keep things confidential, so you don't have to worry about anything getting back to your employer or coworkers. You can review the limits of confidentiality and privacy with your provider at any time.

Sometimes when a difficult experience involves discrimination or violence due to your race, ethnicity, gender, or sexual orientation, it can be especially difficult to move on. Connecting with community action and support groups focused on these issues can sometimes be a part of the healing process. In addition, some people find that social action in response to discrimination can help them move through the difficult experience and into a place of feeling empowered. If your rights have been violated, you may want to seek legal counsel. If they were violated at work, you may want to report it to Human Resources (HR).

Appendix C, "Additional Resources," has some specific resources that may be helpful.

Over the course of our careers, we are happy to have been able to help so many people who have been through difficult experiences. We are proud of you for deciding to work on yours. We sincerely hope that this workbook has helped in your journey. We are all works in progress. Good luck in yours!

APPENDIX A

Worksheets

The printed worksheets for all activities in this workbook appear in the chapters in which they are discussed and again all together in this appendix. They can also be accessed by searching for this book's title on the Oxford Academic platform, at academic.oup.com. For the memory processing work, you may use the worksheets in this workbook or you may choose to audio-record the memory using the Messy Memories app, available from the Apple App Store or Google Play.

In this appendix, we provide enough worksheets for 6 weeks of practice, but please feel free to work at your own pace and make copies of worksheets or add paper if you need more.

WORKSHEET 3.1: Mood Thermometers

Date: _____

Make a mark on each line that describes how you have been feeling on *average* over the *past week*. We suggest you complete a new version of this worksheet once per week while working on the program.

```
0---------1---------2---------3---------4---------5---------6---------7---------8---------9--------10
Calm                                         Neutral                                        Anxious
```

```
0---------1---------2---------3---------4---------5---------6---------7---------8---------9--------10
Happy                                        Neutral                                           Sad
```

```
0---------1---------2---------3---------4---------5---------6---------7---------8---------9--------10
Peaceful                                     Neutral                                        Angry
```

```
0---------1---------2---------3---------4---------5---------6---------7---------8---------9--------10
Organized                                    Neutral                                  Disorganized
```

```
0---------1---------2---------3---------4---------5---------6---------7---------8---------9--------10
Socially Connected                           Neutral                                     Isolated
```

```
0---------1---------2---------3---------4---------5---------6---------7---------8---------9--------10
Proud                                        Neutral                                      Ashamed
```

WORKSHEET 3.1: Mood Thermometers

Date: _____

Make a mark on each line that describes how you have been feeling on *average* over the *past week*. We suggest you complete a new version of this worksheet once per week while working on the program.

```
0---------1---------2---------3---------4---------5---------6---------7---------8---------9--------10
Calm                                    Neutral                                         Anxious
```

```
0---------1---------2---------3---------4---------5---------6---------7---------8---------9--------10
Happy                                   Neutral                                             Sad
```

```
0---------1---------2---------3---------4---------5---------6---------7---------8---------9--------10
Peaceful                                Neutral                                           Angry
```

```
0---------1---------2---------3---------4---------5---------6---------7---------8---------9--------10
Organized                               Neutral                                     Disorganized
```

```
0---------1---------2---------3---------4---------5---------6---------7---------8---------9--------10
Socially Connected                      Neutral                                        Isolated
```

```
0---------1---------2---------3---------4---------5---------6---------7---------8---------9--------10
Proud                                   Neutral                                         Ashamed
```

WORKSHEET 3.1: Mood Thermometers

Date: _____

Make a mark on each line that describes how you have been feeling on *average* over the *past week*. We suggest you complete a new version of this worksheet once per week while working on the program.

0---------1----------2----------3----------4----------5----------6----------7----------8----------9---------10
Calm   Neutral   Anxious

0---------1----------2----------3----------4----------5----------6----------7----------8----------9---------10
Happy   Neutral   Sad

0---------1----------2----------3----------4----------5----------6----------7----------8----------9---------10
Peaceful   Neutral   Angry

0---------1----------2----------3----------4----------5----------6----------7----------8----------9---------10
Organized   Neutral   Disorganized

0---------1----------2----------3----------4----------5----------6----------7----------8----------9---------10
Socially Connected   Neutral   Isolated

0---------1----------2----------3----------4----------5----------6----------7----------8----------9---------10
Proud   Neutral   Ashamed

WORKSHEET 3.1: Mood Thermometers

Date: _____

Make a mark on each line that describes how you have been feeling on average over the past week. We suggest you complete a new version of this worksheet once per week while working on the program.

0---------1----------2----------3----------4---------5----------6---------7----------8----------9---------10
Calm   Neutral   Anxious

0---------1---------2----------3----------4---------5----------6---------7----------8----------9---------10
Happy   Neutral   Sad

0---------1---------2----------3----------4---------5----------6---------7----------8----------9---------10
Peaceful   Neutral   Angry

0---------1---------2----------3----------4---------5----------6---------7----------8----------9---------10
Organized   Neutral   Disorganized

0---------1---------2----------3----------4---------5----------6---------7----------8----------9---------10
Socially Connected   Neutral   Isolated

0---------1---------2----------3----------4---------5----------6---------7----------8----------9---------10
Proud   Neutral   Ashamed

WORKSHEET 3.1: Mood Thermometers

Date: _____

Make a mark on each line that describes how you have been feeling on *average* over the *past week*. We suggest you complete a new version of this worksheet once per week while working on the program.

O---------1----------2----------3----------4----------5----------6---------7----------8----------9---------10
Calm   Neutral   Anxious

O---------1----------2----------3----------4----------5----------6---------7----------8----------9---------10
Happy   Neutral   Sad

O---------1----------2----------3----------4----------5----------6---------7----------8----------9---------10
Peaceful   Neutral   Angry

O---------1----------2----------3----------4----------5----------6---------7----------8----------9---------10
Organized   Neutral   Disorganized

O---------1----------2----------3----------4----------5----------6---------7----------8----------9---------10
Socially Connected   Neutral   Isolated

O---------1----------2----------3----------4----------5----------6---------7----------8----------9---------10
Proud   Neutral   Ashamed

WORKSHEET 3.1: Mood Thermometers

Date: _____

Make a mark on each line that describes how you have been feeling on *average* over the *past week*. We suggest you complete a new version of this worksheet once per week while working on the program.

```
0---------1---------2---------3---------4---------5---------6---------7---------8---------9--------10
Calm                                    Neutral                                          Anxious
```

```
0---------1---------2---------3---------4---------5---------6---------7---------8---------9--------10
Happy                                   Neutral                                             Sad
```

```
0---------1---------2---------3---------4---------5---------6---------7---------8---------9--------10
Peaceful                                Neutral                                           Angry
```

```
0---------1---------2---------3---------4---------5---------6---------7---------8---------9--------10
Organized                               Neutral                                     Disorganized
```

```
0---------1---------2---------3---------4---------5---------6---------7---------8---------9--------10
Socially Connected                      Neutral                                        Isolated
```

```
0---------1---------2---------3---------4---------5---------6---------7---------8---------9--------10
Proud                                   Neutral                                        Ashamed
```

WORKSHEET 3.2: Difficult Experience Writing Exercise

Date: _____

Rate your distress right BEFORE completing the difficult experience exercise:

0---------1---------2----------3----------4---------5----------6---------7----------8----------9---------10
Completely Relaxed   Noticeably Upset   Most Distressed Ever

Describe your difficult experience below. Begin from the moment in the memory when you feel it getting difficult or messy and end at the moment when you feel the immediate risk or event is over. Include all the details that let you connect with the memory, including what you see, what you feel in your body, what you think, and how the details unfold. Let yourself feel the emotions as they come up. Do not avoid or push them away. Revisit the memory by writing in the present tense as though it is happening now. When you finish writing it out once, review it twice or for 20 to 30 minutes, whichever is longer. Please feel free to use additional pages.

_____

_____

_____

_____

_____

_____

_____

_____

_____

_____

_____

_____

_____

_____

_____

_____

_____

_____

_____

_____

_____

_____

_____

_____

_____

_____

_____

_____

_____

_____

_____

_____

How long did you work on the difficult experience exercise? _____ minutes

Rate your distress right AFTER completing the difficult experience exercise:
0----------1----------2----------3----------4----------5----------6----------7----------8----------9---------10
Completely Relaxed   Noticeably Upset   Most Distressed Ever

Rate the HIGHEST level of your distress during the difficult experience exercise:
0----------1----------2----------3----------4----------5----------6----------7----------8----------9---------10
Completely Relaxed   Noticeably Upset   Most Distressed Ever

Review Worksheet 3.2: Difficult Experience Writing Exercise, at least three times per week or even daily if you would like. For each review, read the memory at least three times or for at least 20 to 30 minutes and complete a record of your review using Worksheet 3.4: Daily Review of the Difficult Experiences Writing Exercise.

WORKSHEET 3.2: Difficult Experience Writing Exercise

Date: _____

Rate your distress right BEFORE completing the difficult experience exercise:

0---------1---------2----------3----------4---------5----------6---------7----------8----------9---------10
Completely Relaxed   Noticeably Upset   Most Distressed Ever

Describe your difficult experience below. Begin from the moment in the memory when you feel it getting difficult or messy and end at the moment when you feel the immediate risk or event is over. Include all the details that let you connect with the memory, including what you see, what you feel in your body, what you think, and how the details unfold. Let yourself feel the emotions as they come up. Do not avoid or push them away. Revisit the memory by writing in the present tense as though it is happening now. When you finish writing it out once, review it twice or for 20 to 30 minutes, whichever is longer. Please feel free to use additional pages.

_____

_____

_____

_____

_____

_____

_____

_____

_____

_____

_____

_____

_____

_____

_____

_____

_____

_____

_____

_____

_____

_____

_____

_____

_____

_____

_____

_____

_____

_____

_____

_____

How long did you work on the difficult experience exercise? _____ minutes

Rate your distress right AFTER completing the difficult experience exercise:

0---------1---------2----------3----------4---------5----------6---------7----------8----------9---------10

Completely Relaxed   Noticeably Upset   Most Distressed Ever

Rate the HIGHEST level of your distress during the difficult experience exercise:

0---------1---------2----------3----------4---------5----------6---------7----------8----------9---------10

Completely Relaxed   Noticeably Upset   Most Distressed Ever

Review Worksheet 3.2: Difficult Experience Writing Exercise, at least three times per week or even daily if you would like. For each review, read the memory at least three times or for at least 20 to 30 minutes and complete a record of your review using Worksheet 3.4: Daily Review of the Difficult Experiences Writing Exercise.

WORKSHEET 3.2: Difficult Experience Writing Exercise

Date: _____

Rate your distress right BEFORE completing the difficult experience exercise:

0---------1---------2----------3----------4---------5----------6---------7----------8----------9---------10
Completely Relaxed   Noticeably Upset   Most Distressed Ever

Describe your difficult experience below. Begin from the moment in the memory when you feel it getting difficult or messy and end at the moment when you feel the immediate risk or event is over. Include all the details that let you connect with the memory, including what you see, what you feel in your body, what you think, and how the details unfold. Let yourself feel the emotions as they come up. Do not avoid or push them away. Revisit the memory by writing in the present tense as though it is happening now. When you finish writing it out once, review it twice or for 20 to 30 minutes, whichever is longer. Please feel free to use additional pages.

_____

_____

_____

_____

_____

_____

_____

_____

_____

_____

_____

_____

_____

_____

_____

_____

_____

_____

_____

_____

_____

_____

_____

_____

_____

_____

_____

_____

_____

_____

_____

How long did you work on the difficult experience exercise? _____ minutes

Rate your distress right AFTER completing the difficult experience exercise:

0---------1---------2----------3----------4---------5----------6---------7----------8----------9---------10

Completely Relaxed   Noticeably Upset   Most Distressed Ever

Rate the HIGHEST level of your distress during the difficult experience exercise:

0---------1---------2----------3----------4---------5----------6---------7----------8----------9---------10

Completely Relaxed   Noticeably Upset   Most Distressed Ever

Review Worksheet 3.2: Difficult Experience Writing Exercise, at least three times per week or even daily if you would like. For each review, read the memory at least three times or for at least 20 to 30 minutes and complete a record of your review using Worksheet 3.4: Daily Review of the Difficult Experiences Writing Exercise.

WORKSHEET 3.2: Difficult Experience Writing Exercise

Date: _____

Rate your distress right BEFORE completing the difficult experience exercise:

0---------1---------2----------3----------4---------5----------6--------7----------8----------9--------10
Completely Relaxed   Noticeably Upset   Most Distressed Ever

Describe your difficult experience below. Begin from the moment in the memory when you feel it getting difficult or messy and end at the moment when you feel the immediate risk or event is over. Include all the details that let you connect with the memory, including what you see, what you feel in your body, what you think, and how the details unfold. Let yourself feel the emotions as they come up. Do not avoid or push them away. Revisit the memory by writing in the present tense as though it is happening now. When you finish writing it out once, review it twice or for 20 to 30 minutes, whichever is longer. Please feel free to use additional pages.

_____

_____

_____

_____

_____

_____

_____

_____

_____

_____

_____

_____

_____

_____

_____

_____

_____

How long did you work on the difficult experience exercise? _____ minutes

Rate your distress right AFTER completing the difficult experience exercise:

0----------1----------2----------3----------4----------5----------6----------7----------8----------9----------10
Completely Relaxed   Noticeably Upset   Most Distressed Ever

Rate the HIGHEST level of your distress during the difficult experience exercise:

0----------1----------2----------3----------4----------5----------6----------7----------8----------9----------10
Completely Relaxed   Noticeably Upset   Most Distressed Ever

Review Worksheet 3.2: Difficult Experience Writing Exercise, at least three times per week or even daily if you would like. For each review, read the memory at least three times or for at least 20 to 30 minutes and complete a record of your review using Worksheet 3.4: Daily Review of the Difficult Experiences Writing Exercise.

WORKSHEET 3.2: Difficult Experience Writing Exercise

Date: _____

Rate your distress right BEFORE completing the difficult experience exercise:

0---------1---------2---------3---------4---------5---------6---------7---------8---------9---------10
Completely Relaxed　　　　　　　　　　Noticeably Upset　　　　　　　　　Most Distressed Ever

Describe your difficult experience below. Begin from the moment in the memory when you feel it getting difficult or messy and end at the moment when you feel the immediate risk or event is over. Include all the details that let you connect with the memory, including what you see, what you feel in your body, what you think, and how the details unfold. Let yourself feel the emotions as they come up. Do not avoid or push them away. Revisit the memory by writing in the present tense as though it is happening now. When you finish writing it out once, review it twice or for 20 to 30 minutes, whichever is longer. Please feel free to use additional pages.

_____

_____

_____

_____

_____

_____

_____

_____

_____

_____

_____

_____

_____

_____

_____

_____

_____

_____

_____

_____

_____

_____

_____

_____

_____

_____

_____

_____

_____

_____

_____

_____

_____

_____

How long did you work on the difficult experience exercise? _____ minutes

Rate your distress right AFTER completing the difficult experience exercise:

0---------1---------2----------3----------4---------5----------6---------7----------8----------9---------10

Completely Relaxed   Noticeably Upset   Most Distressed Ever

Rate the HIGHEST level of your distress during the difficult experience exercise:

0---------1---------2----------3----------4---------5----------6---------7----------8----------9---------10

Completely Relaxed   Noticeably Upset   Most Distressed Ever

Review Worksheet 3.2: Difficult Experience Writing Exercise, at least three times per week or even daily if you would like. For each review, read the memory at least three times or for at least 20 to 30 minutes and complete a record of your review using Worksheet 3.4: Daily Review of the Difficult Experiences Writing Exercise.

WORKSHEET 3.2: Difficult Experience Writing Exercise

Date: _____

Rate your distress right BEFORE completing the difficult experience exercise:

0---------1---------2----------3----------4---------5----------6---------7----------8----------9---------10
Completely Relaxed   Noticeably Upset   Most Distressed Ever

Describe your difficult experience below. Begin from the moment in the memory when you feel it getting difficult or messy and end at the moment when you feel the immediate risk or event is over. Include all the details that let you connect with the memory, including what you see, what you feel in your body, what you think, and how the details unfold. Let yourself feel the emotions as they come up. Do not avoid or push them away. Revisit the memory by writing in the present tense as though it is happening now. When you finish writing it out once, review it twice or for 20 to 30 minutes, whichever is longer. Please feel free to use additional pages.

_____

_____

_____

_____

_____

_____

_____

_____

_____

_____

_____

_____

_____

_____

_____

_____

_____

_____

_____

_____

_____

_____

_____

_____

_____

_____

_____

_____

_____

_____

_____

_____

How long did you work on the difficult experience exercise? _____ minutes

Rate your distress right AFTER completing the difficult experience exercise:
0---------1---------2----------3----------4---------5----------6---------7----------8----------9---------10
Completely Relaxed   Noticeably Upset   Most Distressed Ever

Rate the HIGHEST level of your distress during the difficult experience exercise:
0---------1---------2----------3----------4---------5----------6---------7----------8----------9---------10
Completely Relaxed   Noticeably Upset   Most Distressed Ever

Review Worksheet 3.2: Difficult Experience Writing Exercise, at least three times per week or even daily if you would like. For each review, read the memory at least three times or for at least 20 to 30 minutes and complete a record of your review using Worksheet 3.4: Daily Review of the Difficult Experiences Writing Exercise.

WORKSHEET 3.3: Difficult Experience Processing Exercise

Please complete this worksheet once weekly and review the processing questions after each 20- to 30-minute difficult experience writing exercise (Worksheet 3.2) or after a difficult experience daily review (Worksheet 3.4). If you need more space for any question, just grab a sheet of paper and keep writing.

1. Why did this happen to you? What was the cause? _____

_____

_____

2. How did the difficult experience change how you think about yourself? _____

_____

_____

3. How did the difficult experience change how you think about others? _____

_____

_____

4. How did the difficult experience change how you see the world? _____

_____

_____

5. After completing Worksheets 3.2 or 3.4, what new, different, or important information did you notice today? _____

_____

6. What would you tell your family member, loved one, or friend if this had happened to them?

_____

_____

WORKSHEET 3.3: Difficult Experience Processing Exercise

Please complete this worksheet once weekly and review the processing questions after each 20- to 30-minute difficult experience writing exercise (Worksheet 3.2) or after a difficult experience daily review (Worksheet 3.4). If you need more space for any question, just grab a sheet of paper and keep writing.

1. Why did this happen to you? What was the cause? _____

_____

_____

2. How did the difficult experience change how you think about yourself? _____

_____

_____

3. How did the difficult experience change how you think about others? _____

_____

_____

4. How did the difficult experience change how you see the world? _____

_____

_____

5. After completing Worksheets 3.2 or 3.4, what new, different, or important information did you notice today? _____

_____

6. What would you tell your family member, loved one, or friend if this had happened to them?

_____

_____

WORKSHEET 3.3: Difficult Experience Processing Exercise

Please complete this worksheet once weekly and review the processing questions after each 20- to 30-minute difficult experience writing exercise (Worksheet 3.2) or after a difficult experience daily review (Worksheet 3.4). If you need more space for any question, just grab a sheet of paper and keep writing.

1. Why did this happen to you? What was the cause? _____

_____

_____

2. How did the difficult experience change how you think about yourself? _____

_____

_____

3. How did the difficult experience change how you think about others? _____

_____

_____

4. How did the difficult experience change how you see the world? _____

_____

_____

5. After completing Worksheets 3.2 or 3.4, what new, different, or important information did you notice today? _____

_____

6. What would you tell your family member, loved one, or friend if this had happened to them?

_____

_____

WORKSHEET 3.3: Difficult Experience Processing Exercise

Please complete this worksheet once weekly and review the processing questions after each 20- to 30-minute difficult experience writing exercise (Worksheet 3.2) or after a difficult experience daily review (Worksheet 3.4). If you need more space for any question, just grab a sheet of paper and keep writing.

1. Why did this happen to you? What was the cause? _____

   _____

   _____

2. How did the difficult experience change how you think about yourself? _____

   _____

   _____

3. How did the difficult experience change how you think about others? _____

   _____

   _____

4. How did the difficult experience change how you see the world? _____

   _____

   _____

5. After completing Worksheets 3.2 or 3.4, what new, different, or important information did you notice today? _____

   _____

6. What would you tell your family member, loved one, or friend if this had happened to them?

   _____

   _____

WORKSHEET 3.3: Difficult Experience Processing Exercise

Please complete this worksheet once weekly and review the processing questions after each 20- to 30-minute difficult experience writing exercise (Worksheet 3.2) or after a difficult experience daily review (Worksheet 3.4). If you need more space for any question, just grab a sheet of paper and keep writing.

1. Why did this happen to you? What was the cause? _____

_____

_____

2. How did the difficult experience change how you think about yourself? _____

_____

_____

3. How did the difficult experience change how you think about others? _____

_____

_____

4. How did the difficult experience change how you see the world? _____

_____

_____

5. After completing Worksheets 3.2 or 3.4, what new, different, or important information did you notice today? _____

_____

6. What would you tell your family member, loved one, or friend if this had happened to them?

_____

_____

WORKSHEET 3.3: Difficult Experience Processing Exercise

Please complete this worksheet once weekly and review the processing questions after each 20- to 30-minute difficult experience writing exercise (Worksheet 3.2) or after a difficult experience daily review (Worksheet 3.4). If you need more space for any question, just grab a sheet of paper and keep writing.

1. Why did this happen to you? What was the cause? _____

_____

_____

2. How did the difficult experience change how you think about yourself? _____

_____

_____

3. How did the difficult experience change how you think about others? _____

_____

_____

4. How did the difficult experience change how you see the world? _____

_____

_____

5. After completing Worksheets 3.2 or 3.4, what new, different, or important information did you notice
   today? _____

_____

6. What would you tell your family member, loved one, or friend if this had happened to them?

_____

_____

WORKSHEET 3.4: Daily Review of the Difficult Experience Writing Exercise

Review Worksheet 3.2: Difficult Experience Writing Exercise at least three times per week or even daily if you would like. For each review, read the memory at least three times or for at least 20 to 30 minutes and complete a record of your review using this Worksheet to record your distress just prior to, during, and just after each difficult experience daily review. Remember, we suggest that each difficult experience daily review includes

1. Reading the difficult memory from the Difficult Experience Writing Exercise (Worksheet 3.2) at least three times or 20 minutes—whichever is longer.
2. Completing a Difficult Experience Processing Exercise (Worksheet 3.3) once per week or reviewing this week's version.
3. Completing your choice of the Exploring Emotions in Your Difficult Experience (Worksheets 3.5 to 3.8) once per week or reviewing this week's version.

Use the following scale to rate your distress:

0---------1---------2----------3----------4---------5----------6---------7----------8----------9---------10
Completely   Mostly   Noticeably   Very   Most Upset
Relaxed   Relaxed   Upset   Upset   Ever

Date of review	Minutes reviewed	Distress level right **BEFORE** reviewing the difficult experience (0–10)	Distress level right **AFTER** reviewing the difficult experience (0–10)	**HIGHEST** level of distress reviewing the difficult experience (0–10)

WORKSHEET 3.4: Daily Review of the Difficult Experience Writing Exercise

Review Worksheet 3.2: Difficult Experience Writing Exercise at least three times per week or even daily if you would like. For each review, read the memory at least three times or for at least 20 to 30 minutes and complete a record of your review using this Worksheet to record your distress just prior to, during, and just after each difficult experience daily review. Remember, we suggest that each difficult experience daily review includes

1. Reading the difficult memory from the Difficult Experience Writing Exercise (Worksheet 3.2) at least three times or 20 minutes—whichever is longer.
2. Completing a Difficult Experience Processing Exercise (Worksheet 3.3) once per week or reviewing this week's version.
3. Completing your choice of the Exploring Emotions in Your Difficult Experience (Worksheets 3.5 to 3.8) once per week or reviewing this week's version.

Use the following scale to rate your distress:

0---------1---------2----------3----------4---------5----------6---------7----------8----------9---------10
Completely
Relaxed

Mostly
Relaxed

Noticeably
Upset

Very
Upset

Most Upset
Ever

Date of review	Minutes reviewed	Distress level right **BEFORE** reviewing the difficult experience (0–10)	Distress level right **AFTER** reviewing the difficult experience (0–10)	**HIGHEST** level of distress reviewing the difficult experience (0–10)

WORKSHEET 3.4: Daily Review of the Difficult Experience Writing Exercise

Review Worksheet 3.2: Difficult Experience Writing Exercise at least three times per week or even daily if you would like. For each review, read the memory at least three times or for at least 20 to 30 minutes and complete a record of your review using this Worksheet to record your distress just prior to, during, and just after each difficult experience daily review. Remember, we suggest that each difficult experience daily review includes

1. Reading the difficult memory from the Difficult Experience Writing Exercise (Worksheet 3.2) at least three times or 20 minutes—whichever is longer.

2. Completing a Difficult Experience Processing Exercise (Worksheet 3.3) once per week or reviewing this week's version.

3. Completing your choice of the Exploring Emotions in Your Difficult Experience (Worksheets 3.5 to 3.8) once per week or reviewing this week's version.

Use the following scale to rate your distress:

0---------1---------2---------3---------4---------5---------6---------7---------8---------9---------10
Completely Relaxed · Mostly Relaxed · Noticeably Upset · Very Upset · Most Upset Ever

Date of review	Minutes reviewed	Distress level right BEFORE reviewing the difficult experience (0–10)	Distress level right AFTER reviewing the difficult experience (0–10)	HIGHEST level of distress reviewing the difficult experience (0–10)

WORKSHEET 3.4: Daily Review of the Difficult Experience Writing Exercise

Review Worksheet 3.2: Difficult Experience Writing Exercise at least three times per week or even daily if you would like. For each review, read the memory at least three times or for at least 20 to 30 minutes and complete a record of your review using this Worksheet to record your distress just prior to, during, and just after each difficult experience daily review. Remember, we suggest that each difficult experience daily review includes

1. Reading the difficult memory from the Difficult Experience Writing Exercise (Worksheet 3.2) at least three times or 20 minutes—whichever is longer.

2. Completing a Difficult Experience Processing Exercise (Worksheet 3.3) once per week or reviewing this week's version.

3. Completing your choice of the Exploring Emotions in Your Difficult Experience (Worksheets 3.5 to 3.8) once per week or reviewing this week's version.

Use the following scale to rate your distress:

0---------1---------2----------3----------4---------5----------6---------7----------8----------9---------10
Completely Relaxed   Mostly Relaxed   Noticeably Upset   Very Upset   Most Upset Ever

Date of review	Minutes reviewed	Distress level right **BEFORE** reviewing the difficult experience (0–10)	Distress level right **AFTER** reviewing the difficult experience (0–10)	**HIGHEST** level of distress reviewing the difficult experience (0–10)

WORKSHEET 3.4: Daily Review of the Difficult Experience Writing Exercise

Review Worksheet 3.2: Difficult Experience Writing Exercise at least three times per week or even daily if you would like. For each review, read the memory at least three times or for at least 20 to 30 minutes and complete a record of your review using this Worksheet to record your distress just prior to, during, and just after each difficult experience daily review. Remember, we suggest that each difficult experience daily review includes

1. Reading the difficult memory from the Difficult Experience Writing Exercise (Worksheet 3.2) at least three times or 20 minutes—whichever is longer.
2. Completing a Difficult Experience Processing Exercise (Worksheet 3.3) once per week or reviewing this week's version.
3. Completing your choice of the Exploring Emotions in Your Difficult Experience (Worksheets 3.5 to 3.8) once per week or reviewing this week's version.

Use the following scale to rate your distress:

0	1	2	3	4	5	6	7	8	9	10
Completely Relaxed			Mostly Relaxed		Noticeably Upset		Very Upset			Most Upset Ever

Date of review	Minutes reviewed	Distress level right **BEFORE** reviewing the difficult experience (0–10)	Distress level right **AFTER** reviewing the difficult experience (0–10)	**HIGHEST** level of distress reviewing the difficult experience (0–10)

WORKSHEET 3.4: Daily Review of the Difficult Experience Writing Exercise

Review Worksheet 3.2: Difficult Experience Writing Exercise at least three times per week or even daily if you would like. For each review, read the memory at least three times or for at least 20 to 30 minutes and complete a record of your review using this Worksheet to record your distress just prior to, during, and just after each difficult experience daily review. Remember, we suggest that each difficult experience daily review includes

1. Reading the difficult memory from the Difficult Experience Writing Exercise (Worksheet 3.2) at least three times or 20 minutes—whichever is longer.

2. Completing a Difficult Experience Processing Exercise (Worksheet 3.3) once per week or reviewing this week's version.

3. Completing your choice of the Exploring Emotions in Your Difficult Experience (Worksheets 3.5 to 3.8) once per week or reviewing this week's version.

Use the following scale to rate your distress:

```
0---------1---------2---------3---------4---------5---------6---------7---------8---------9---------10
Completely                Mostly          Noticeably        Very                      Most Upset
Relaxed                   Relaxed         Upset             Upset                     Ever
```

Date of review	Minutes reviewed	Distress level right BEFORE reviewing the difficult experience (0–10)	Distress level right AFTER reviewing the difficult experience (0–10)	HIGHEST level of distress reviewing the difficult experience (0–10)

WORSHEET 3.5: Exploring Emotions in Your Difficult Experience:

SADNESS

Please choose which Exploring Emotions in Your Difficult Experience worksheet/s (Worksheets 3.5 to 3.8) you want to review after each 20- to 30-minute difficult experience writing exercise (Worksheet 3.2) OR difficult experience daily review (Worksheet 3.4). Complete this worksheet once weekly and review it with each daily review. If you need more space for any question, just grab a sheet of paper and keep writing.

1. Do you feel like this sadness is similar to how most people would be feeling at this point since the event?   YES   NO   I AM NOT SURE

If you answered YES, letting yourself grieve this loss or situation makes sense. Letting yourself feel sadness can often be the best way to move through sadness to the other side. What can you do to care for yourself while you grieve? _____

_____

If you answered NO or I AM NOT SURE, why do you think this level of sadness is sticking with you?

_____

_____

2. Are you ready to let the sadness go?   YES   NO   I AM NOT SURE

If you answered NO or I AM NOT SURE, what do you need to be ready to let the sadness go? HINT: Only YOU can decide when to let the sadness go. _____

_____

If you answered YES, then let it go. HINT: Deciding to let it go does not mean it is OK that it happened, just that you are deciding not to carry the sadness with you.

WORKSHEET 3.5: Exploring Emotions in Your Difficult Experience:

SADNESS

Please choose which Exploring Emotions in Your Difficult Experience worksheet/s (Worksheets 3.5 to 3.8) you want to review after each 20- to 30-minute difficult experience writing exercise (Worksheet 3.2) OR difficult experience daily review (Worksheet 3.4). Complete this worksheet once weekly and review it with each daily review. If you need more space for any question, just grab a sheet of paper and keep writing.

1. Do you feel like this sadness is similar to how most people would be feeling at this point since the event?   YES   NO   I AM NOT SURE

If you answered YES, letting yourself grieve this loss or situation makes sense. Letting yourself feel sadness can often be the best way to move through sadness to the other side. What can you do to care for yourself while you grieve? _____

_____

If you answered NO or I AM NOT SURE, why do you think this level of sadness is sticking with you?

_____

_____

2. Are you ready to let the sadness go?   YES   NO   I AM NOT SURE

If you answered NO or I AM NOT SURE, what do you need to be ready to let the sadness go? HINT: Only YOU can decide when to let the sadness go. _____

_____

If you answered YES, then let it go. HINT: Deciding to let it go does not mean it is OK that it happened, just that you are deciding not to carry the sadness with you.

WORKSHEET 3.5: Exploring Emotions in Your Difficult Experience:

SADNESS

Please choose which Exploring Emotions in Your Difficult Experience worksheet/s (Worksheets 3.5 to 3.8) you want to review after each 20- to 30-minute difficult experience writing exercise (Worksheet 3.2) OR difficult experience daily review (Worksheet 3.4). Complete this worksheet once weekly and review it with each daily review. If you need more space for any question, just grab a sheet of paper and keep writing.

1. Do you feel like this sadness is similar to how most people would be feeling at this point since the event?   YES   NO   I AM NOT SURE

If you answered YES, letting yourself grieve this loss or situation makes sense. Letting yourself feel sadness can often be the best way to move through sadness to the other side. What can you do to care for yourself while you grieve? _____

_____

If you answered NO or I AM NOT SURE, why do you think this level of sadness is sticking with you?

_____

_____

2. Are you ready to let the sadness go?   YES   NO   I AM NOT SURE

If you answered NO or I AM NOT SURE, what do you need to be ready to let the sadness go? HINT: Only YOU can decide when to let the sadness go. _____

_____

If you answered YES, then let it go. HINT: Deciding to let it go does not mean it is OK that it happened, just that you are deciding not to carry the sadness with you.

WORKSHEET 3.5: Exploring Emotions in Your Difficult Experience:

SADNESS

Please choose which Exploring Emotions in Your Difficult Experience worksheet/s (Worksheets 3.5 to 3.8) you want to review after each 20- to 30-minute difficult experience writing exercise (Worksheet 3.2) OR difficult experience daily review (Worksheet 3.4). Complete this worksheet once weekly and review it with each daily review. If you need more space for any question, just grab a sheet of paper and keep writing.

1. Do you feel like this sadness is similar to how most people would be feeling at this point since the event?   YES   NO   I AM NOT SURE

If you answered YES, letting yourself grieve this loss or situation makes sense. Letting yourself feel sadness can often be the best way to move through sadness to the other side. What can you do to care for yourself while you grieve? _____

_____

If you answered NO or I AM NOT SURE, why do you think this level of sadness is sticking with you?

_____

_____

2. Are you ready to let the sadness go?   YES   NO   I AM NOT SURE

If you answered NO or I AM NOT SURE, what do you need to be ready to let the sadness go? HINT: Only YOU can decide when to let the sadness go. _____

_____

If you answered YES, then let it go. HINT: Deciding to let it go does not mean it is OK that it happened, just that you are deciding not to carry the sadness with you.

WORKSHEET 3.5: Exploring Emotions in Your Difficult Experience:

SADNESS

Please choose which Exploring Emotions in Your Difficult Experience worksheet/s (Worksheets 3.5 to 3.8) you want to review after each 20- to 30-minute difficult experience writing exercise (Worksheet 3.2) OR difficult experience daily review (Worksheet 3.4). Complete this worksheet once weekly and review it with each daily review. If you need more space for any question, just grab a sheet of paper and keep writing.

1. Do you feel like this sadness is similar to how most people would be feeling at this point since the event?   YES   NO   I AM NOT SURE

If you answered YES, letting yourself grieve this loss or situation makes sense. Letting yourself feel sadness can often be the best way to move through sadness to the other side. What can you do to care for yourself while you grieve? _____

_____

If you answered NO or I AM NOT SURE, why do you think this level of sadness is sticking with you?

_____

_____

2. Are you ready to let the sadness go?   YES   NO   I AM NOT SURE

If you answered NO or I AM NOT SURE, what do you need to be ready to let the sadness go? HINT: Only YOU can decide when to let the sadness go. _____

_____

If you answered YES, then let it go. HINT: Deciding to let it go does not mean it is OK that it happened, just that you are deciding not to carry the sadness with you.

WORKSHEET 3.5: Exploring Emotions in Your Difficult Experience:

SADNESS

Please choose which Exploring Emotions in Your Difficult Experience worksheet/s (Worksheets 3.5 to 3.8) you want to review after each 20- to 30-minute difficult experience writing exercise (Worksheet 3.2) OR difficult experience daily review (Worksheet 3.4). Complete this worksheet once weekly and review it with each daily review. If you need more space for any question, just grab a sheet of paper and keep writing.

1. Do you feel like this sadness is similar to how most people would be feeling at this point since the event?   YES   NO   I AM NOT SURE

If you answered YES, letting yourself grieve this loss or situation makes sense. Letting yourself feel sadness can often be the best way to move through sadness to the other side. What can you do to care for yourself while you grieve? _____

_____

If you answered NO or I AM NOT SURE, why do you think this level of sadness is sticking with you?

_____

_____

2. Are you ready to let the sadness go?   YES   NO   I AM NOT SURE

If you answered NO or I AM NOT SURE, what do you need to be ready to let the sadness go? HINT: Only YOU can decide when to let the sadness go. _____

_____

If you answered YES, then let it go. HINT: Deciding to let it go does not mean it is OK that it happened, just that you are deciding not to carry the sadness with you.

WORKSHEET 3.6: Exploring Emotions in Your Difficult Experience:

FEAR or ANXIETY

Please choose which Exploring Emotions in Your Difficult Experience sheet/s (Worksheets 3.5 to 3.8) you want to review after each 20- to 30-minute difficult experience writing exercise (Worksheet 3.2) OR difficult experience daily review (Worksheet 3.4). Complete this worksheet once weekly and review it with each daily review. If you need more space for any question, just grab a sheet of paper and keep writing.

1. What are you afraid of or anxious about? _____

_____

2. What is the actual threat now? _____

_____

3. Are you more anxious or afraid than you think most people would be?

      YES   NO   I AM NOT SURE

If you answered YES, why do you think you may be more afraid or anxious than others are?

_____

_____

If you answered NO or I AM NOT SURE, describe below what you need to do to protect yourself. If you cannot think of anything, then the fear may be more than it needs to be now.

_____

_____

4. Are you ready to let the fear and anxiety go?

      YES   NO   I AM NOT SURE

If you answered NO or I AM NOT SURE, what do you need to be ready to let the fear or anxiety go? HINT: Only YOU can decide when to let the fear or anxiety go. _____

_____

If you answered YES, then let it go. HINT: Deciding to let it go does not mean it is OK that it happened, just that you are deciding not to carry the fear and anxiety with you.

WORKSHEET 3.6: Exploring Emotions in Your Difficult Experience:

FEAR or ANXIETY

Please choose which Exploring Emotions in Your Difficult Experience sheet/s (Worksheets 3.5 to 3.8) you want to review after each 20- to 30-minute difficult experience writing exercise (Worksheet 3.2) OR difficult experience daily review (Worksheet 3.4). Complete this worksheet once weekly and review it with each daily review. If you need more space for any question, just grab a sheet of paper and keep writing.

1. What are you afraid of or anxious about? _____

_____

2. What is the actual threat now? _____

_____

3. Are you more anxious or afraid than you think most people would be?

     YES   NO   I AM NOT SURE

If you answered YES, why do you think you may be more afraid or anxious than others are?

_____

_____

If you answered NO or I AM NOT SURE, describe below what you need to do to protect yourself. If you cannot think of anything, then the fear may be more than it needs to be now.

_____

_____

4. Are you ready to let the fear and anxiety go?

     YES   NO   I AM NOT SURE

If you answered NO or I AM NOT SURE, what do you need to be ready to let the fear or anxiety go? HINT: Only YOU can decide when to let the fear or anxiety go. _____

_____

If you answered YES, then let it go. HINT: Deciding to let it go does not mean it is OK that it happened, just that you are deciding not to carry the fear and anxiety with you.

WORKSHEET 3.6: Exploring Emotions in Your Difficult Experience:

FEAR or ANXIETY

Please choose which Exploring Emotions in Your Difficult Experience sheet/s (Worksheets 3.5 to 3.8) you want to review after each 20- to 30-minute difficult experience writing exercise (Worksheet 3.2) OR difficult experience daily review (Worksheet 3.4). Complete this worksheet once weekly and review it with each daily review. If you need more space for any question, just grab a sheet of paper and keep writing.

1. What are you afraid of or anxious about? _____

_____

2. What is the actual threat now? _____

_____

3. Are you more anxious or afraid than you think most people would be?

      YES   NO   I AM NOT SURE

If you answered YES, why do you think you may be more afraid or anxious than others are?

_____

_____

If you answered NO or I AM NOT SURE, describe below what you need to do to protect yourself. If you cannot think of anything, then the fear may be more than it needs to be now.

_____

_____

4. Are you ready to let the fear and anxiety go?

      YES   NO   I AM NOT SURE

If you answered NO or I AM NOT SURE, what do you need to be ready to let the fear or anxiety go? HINT: Only YOU can decide when to let the fear or anxiety go. _____

_____

If you answered YES, then let it go. HINT: Deciding to let it go does not mean it is OK that it happened, just that you are deciding not to carry the fear and anxiety with you.

WORKSHEET 3.6: Exploring Emotions in Your Difficult Experience:

FEAR or ANXIETY

Please choose which Exploring Emotions in Your Difficult Experience sheet/s (Worksheets 3.5 to 3.8) you want to review after each 20- to 30-minute difficult experience writing exercise (Worksheet 3.2) OR difficult experience daily review (Worksheet 3.4). Complete this worksheet once weekly and review it with each daily review. If you need more space for any question, just grab a sheet of paper and keep writing.

1. What are you afraid of or anxious about? _____

_____

2. What is the actual threat now? _____

_____

3. Are you more anxious or afraid than you think most people would be?

      YES   NO   I AM NOT SURE

If you answered YES, why do you think you may be more afraid or anxious than others are?

_____

_____

If you answered NO or I AM NOT SURE, describe below what you need to do to protect yourself. If you cannot think of anything, then the fear may be more than it needs to be now.

_____

_____

4. Are you ready to let the fear and anxiety go?

      YES   NO   I AM NOT SURE

If you answered NO or I AM NOT SURE, what do you need to be ready to let the fear or anxiety go? HINT: Only YOU can decide when to let the fear or anxiety go. _____

_____

If you answered YES, then let it go. HINT: Deciding to let it go does not mean it is OK that it happened, just that you are deciding not to carry the fear and anxiety with you.

WORKSHEET 3.6: Exploring Emotions in Your Difficult Experience:

FEAR or ANXIETY

Please choose which Exploring Emotions in Your Difficult Experience sheet/s (Worksheets 3.5 to 3.8) you want to review after each 20- to 30-minute difficult experience writing exercise (Worksheet 3.2) OR difficult experience daily review (Worksheet 3.4). Complete this worksheet once weekly and review it with each daily review. If you need more space for any question, just grab a sheet of paper and keep writing.

1. What are you afraid of or anxious about? _____

_____

2. What is the actual threat now? _____

_____

3. Are you more anxious or afraid than you think most people would be?

> YES   NO   I AM NOT SURE

If you answered YES, why do you think you may be more afraid or anxious than others are?

_____

_____

If you answered NO or I AM NOT SURE, describe below what you need to do to protect yourself. If you cannot think of anything, then the fear may be more than it needs to be now.

_____

_____

4. Are you ready to let the fear and anxiety go?

> YES   NO   I AM NOT SURE

If you answered NO or I AM NOT SURE, what do you need to be ready to let the fear or anxiety go? HINT: Only YOU can decide when to let the fear or anxiety go. _____

_____

If you answered YES, then let it go. HINT: Deciding to let it go does not mean it is OK that it happened, just that you are deciding not to carry the fear and anxiety with you.

WORKSHEET 3.6: Exploring Emotions in Your Difficult Experience:

FEAR or ANXIETY

Please choose which Exploring Emotions in Your Difficult Experience sheet/s (Worksheets 3.5 to 3.8) you want to review after each 20- to 30-minute difficult experience writing exercise (Worksheet 3.2) OR difficult experience daily review (Worksheet 3.4). Complete this worksheet once weekly and review it with each daily review. If you need more space for any question, just grab a sheet of paper and keep writing.

1. What are you afraid of or anxious about? _____

_____

2. What is the actual threat now? _____

_____

3. Are you more anxious or afraid than you think most people would be?

    YES   NO   I AM NOT SURE

If you answered YES, why do you think you may be more afraid or anxious than others are?

_____

_____

If you answered NO or I AM NOT SURE, describe below what you need to do to protect yourself. If you cannot think of anything, then the fear may be more than it needs to be now.

_____

_____

4. Are you ready to let the fear and anxiety go?

    YES   NO   I AM NOT SURE

If you answered NO or I AM NOT SURE, what do you need to be ready to let the fear or anxiety go? HINT: Only YOU can decide when to let the fear or anxiety go. _____

_____

If you answered YES, then let it go. HINT: Deciding to let it go does not mean it is OK that it happened, just that you are deciding not to carry the fear and anxiety with you.

WORKSHEET 3.7: Exploring Emotions in Your Difficult Experience:

ANGER

Please choose which Exploring Emotions in Your Difficult Experience sheet/s (Worksheets 3.5 to 3.8) you want to review after each 20- to 30-minute difficult experience writing exercise (Worksheet 3.2) OR difficult experience daily review (Worksheet 3.4). Complete this worksheet once weekly and review it with each daily review. If you need more space for any question, just grab a sheet of paper and keep writing.

1. What are you angry, frustrated, or resentful about? _____

_____

_____

2. Holding on to anger can keep you stuck in the memory and feeling like a victim rather than a survivor. This is true even when you may have good reasons to be angry at someone or something that happened. Are you ready to let the anger/frustration/resentment go?

     YES   NO   I AM NOT SURE

If you answered NO or I AM NOT SURE, what do you need to be ready to let the anger/frustration/resentment go? HINT: Only YOU can decide when to let the anger go.

_____

_____

If you answered YES, then let it go. HINT: Deciding to let it go does not mean it is OK that it happened, just that you are deciding not to carry the anger, frustration, or resentment with you.

WORKSHEET 3.7: Exploring Emotions in Your Difficult Experience:

ANGER

Please choose which Exploring Emotions in Your Difficult Experience sheet/s (Worksheets 3.5 to 3.8) you want to review after each 20- to 30-minute difficult experience writing exercise (Worksheet 3.2) OR difficult experience daily review (Worksheet 3.4). Complete this worksheet once weekly and review it with each daily review. If you need more space for any question, just grab a sheet of paper and keep writing.

1. What are you angry, frustrated, or resentful about? _____

_____

_____

2. Holding on to anger can keep you stuck in the memory and feeling like a victim rather than a survivor. This is true even when you may have good reasons to be angry at someone or something that happened. Are you ready to let the anger/frustration/resentment go?

     YES   NO   I AM NOT SURE

If you answered NO or I AM NOT SURE, what do you need to be ready to let the anger/frustration/resentment go? HINT: Only YOU can decide when to let the anger go.

_____

_____

If you answered YES, then let it go. HINT: Deciding to let it go does not mean it is OK that it happened, just that you are deciding not to carry the anger, frustration, or resentment with you.

WORKSHEET 3.7: Exploring Emotions in Your Difficult Experience:

ANGER

Please choose which Exploring Emotions in Your Difficult Experience sheet/s (Worksheets 3.5 to 3.8) you want to review after each 20- to 30-minute difficult experience writing exercise (Worksheet 3.2) OR difficult experience daily review (Worksheet 3.4). Complete this worksheet once weekly and review it with each daily review. If you need more space for any question, just grab a sheet of paper and keep writing.

1. What are you angry, frustrated, or resentful about? _____

_____

_____

2. Holding on to anger can keep you stuck in the memory and feeling like a victim rather than a survivor. This is true even when you may have good reasons to be angry at someone or something that happened. Are you ready to let the anger/frustration/resentment go?

      YES   NO   I AM NOT SURE

If you answered NO or I AM NOT SURE, what do you need to be ready to let the anger/frustration/resentment go? HINT: Only YOU can decide when to let the anger go.

_____

_____

If you answered YES, then let it go. HINT: Deciding to let it go does not mean it is OK that it happened, just that you are deciding not to carry the anger, frustration, or resentment with you.

WORKSHEET 3.7: Exploring Emotions in Your Difficult Experience:

ANGER

Please choose which Exploring Emotions in Your Difficult Experience sheet/s (Worksheets 3.5 to 3.8) you want to review after each 20- to 30-minute difficult experience writing exercise (Worksheet 3.2) OR difficult experience daily review (Worksheet 3.4). Complete this worksheet once weekly and review it with each daily review. If you need more space for any question, just grab a sheet of paper and keep writing.

1. What are you angry, frustrated, or resentful about? _____

_____

_____

2. Holding on to anger can keep you stuck in the memory and feeling like a victim rather than a survivor. This is true even when you may have good reasons to be angry at someone or something that happened. Are you ready to let the anger/frustration/resentment go?

    YES   NO   I AM NOT SURE

If you answered NO or I AM NOT SURE, what do you need to be ready to let the anger/frustration/resentment go? HINT: Only YOU can decide when to let the anger go.

_____

_____

If you answered YES, then let it go. HINT: Deciding to let it go does not mean it is OK that it happened, just that you are deciding not to carry the anger, frustration, or resentment with you.

WORKSHEET 3.7: Exploring Emotions in Your Difficult Experience:

ANGER

Please choose which Exploring Emotions in Your Difficult Experience sheet/s (Worksheets 3.5 to 3.8) you want to review after each 20- to 30-minute difficult experience writing exercise (Worksheet 3.2) OR difficult experience daily review (Worksheet 3.4). Complete this worksheet once weekly and review it with each daily review. If you need more space for any question, just grab a sheet of paper and keep writing.

1. What are you angry, frustrated, or resentful about? _____

_____

_____

2. Holding on to anger can keep you stuck in the memory and feeling like a victim rather than a survivor. This is true even when you may have good reasons to be angry at someone or something that happened. Are you ready to let the anger/frustration/resentment go?

    YES   NO   I AM NOT SURE

If you answered NO or I AM NOT SURE, what do you need to be ready to let the anger/frustration/resentment go? HINT: Only YOU can decide when to let the anger go.

_____

_____

If you answered YES, then let it go. HINT: Deciding to let it go does not mean it is OK that it happened, just that you are deciding not to carry the anger, frustration, or resentment with you.

WORKSHEET 3.7: Exploring Emotions in Your Difficult Experience:

ANGER

Please choose which Exploring Emotions in Your Difficult Experience sheet/s (Worksheets 3.5 to 3.8) you want to review after each 20- to 30-minute difficult experience writing exercise (Worksheet 3.2) OR difficult experience daily review (Worksheet 3.4). Complete this worksheet once weekly and review it with each daily review. If you need more space for any question, just grab a sheet of paper and keep writing.

1. What are you angry, frustrated, or resentful about? _____

_____

_____

2. Holding on to anger can keep you stuck in the memory and feeling like a victim rather than a survivor. This is true even when you may have good reasons to be angry at someone or something that happened. Are you ready to let the anger/frustration/resentment go?

      YES   NO   I AM NOT SURE

If you answered NO or I AM NOT SURE, what do you need to be ready to let the anger/frustration/resentment go? HINT: Only YOU can decide when to let the anger go.

_____

_____

If you answered YES, then let it go. HINT: Deciding to let it go does not mean it is OK that it happened, just that you are deciding not to carry the anger, frustration, or resentment with you.

WORKSHEET 3.8: Exploring Emotions in Your Difficult Experience:

GUILT

Please choose which Exploring Emotions in Your Difficult Experience sheet/s (Worksheets 3.5 to 3.8) you want to review after each 20- to 30-minute difficult experience writing exercise (Worksheet 3.2) OR difficult experience daily review (Worksheet 3.4). Complete this worksheet once weekly and review it with each daily review. If you need more space for any question, just grab a sheet of paper and keep writing.

1. What do you feel guilty about from the difficult experience? _____

_____

_____

2. Holding on to guilt can keep you stuck in the memory and feeling responsible for something you could not control. Are you ready to let the guilt go?

      YES   NO   I AM NOT SURE

If you answered YES, then let it go. HINT: Deciding to let it go does not mean it is OK that it happened, just that you are deciding not to carry the guilt with you any longer.

If you answered NO or I AM NOT SURE, what do you need to do to be ready to let the guilt go? When a situation turns out badly, we all wish we could have done something to have it turn out better.

3. What percentage was your responsibility? HINT: Only YOU can decide when to let the guilt go.

_____

_____

4. If you wish you had done something differently, why didn't you? What aspects of the difficult experience context impacted the choices you made at the time? Even if you were partly responsible for what happened, did anyone else also have some responsibility? _____

_____

_____

5. If your family member, loved one, or friend came to you to talk about feeling guilty about a difficult experience like what you went through, what would you say to them? _____

_____

_____

WORKSHEET 3.8: Exploring Emotions in Your Difficult Experience:

GUILT

Please choose which Exploring Emotions in Your Difficult Experience sheet/s (Worksheets 3.5 to 3.8) you want to review after each 20- to 30-minute difficult experience writing exercise (Worksheet 3.2) OR difficult experience daily review (Worksheet 3.4). Complete this worksheet once weekly and review it with each daily review. If you need more space for any question, just grab a sheet of paper and keep writing.

1. What do you feel guilty about from the difficult experience? _____

_____

_____

2. Holding on to guilt can keep you stuck in the memory and feeling responsible for something you could not control. Are you ready to let the guilt go?

         YES   NO   I AM NOT SURE

If you answered YES, then let it go. HINT: Deciding to let it go does not mean it is OK that it happened, just that you are deciding not to carry the guilt with you any longer.

If you answered NO or I AM NOT SURE, what do you need to do to be ready to let the guilt go? When a situation turns out badly, we all wish we could have done something to have it turn out better.

3. What percentage was your responsibility? HINT: Only YOU can decide when to let the guilt go.

_____

_____

4. If you wish you had done something differently, why didn't you? What aspects of the difficult experience context impacted the choices you made at the time? Even if you were partly responsible for what happened, did anyone else also have some responsibility? _____

_____

_____

5. If your family member, loved one, or friend came to you to talk about feeling guilty about a difficult experience like what you went through, what would you say to them? _____

_____

_____

WORKSHEET 3.8: Exploring Emotions in Your Difficult Experience:

GUILT

Please choose which Exploring Emotions in Your Difficult Experience sheet/s (Worksheets 3.5 to 3.8) you want to review after each 20- to 30-minute difficult experience writing exercise (Worksheet 3.2) OR difficult experience daily review (Worksheet 3.4). Complete this worksheet once weekly and review it with each daily review. If you need more space for any question, just grab a sheet of paper and keep writing.

1. What do you feel guilty about from the difficult experience? _____

_____

_____

2. Holding on to guilt can keep you stuck in the memory and feeling responsible for something you could not control. Are you ready to let the guilt go?

      YES   NO   I AM NOT SURE

If you answered YES, then let it go. HINT: Deciding to let it go does not mean it is OK that it happened, just that you are deciding not to carry the guilt with you any longer.

If you answered NO or I AM NOT SURE, what do you need to do to be ready to let the guilt go? When a situation turns out badly, we all wish we could have done something to have it turn out better.

3. What percentage was your responsibility? HINT: Only YOU can decide when to let the guilt go.

_____

_____

4. If you wish you had done something differently, why didn't you? What aspects of the difficult experience context impacted the choices you made at the time? Even if you were partly responsible for what happened, did anyone else also have some responsibility? _____

_____

_____

5. If your family member, loved one, or friend came to you to talk about feeling guilty about a difficult experience like what you went through, what would you say to them? _____

_____

_____

WORKSHEET 3.8: Exploring Emotions in Your Difficult Experience:

GUILT

Please choose which Exploring Emotions in Your Difficult Experience sheet/s (Worksheets 3.5 to 3.8) you want to review after each 20- to 30-minute difficult experience writing exercise (Worksheet 3.2) OR difficult experience daily review (Worksheet 3.4). Complete this worksheet once weekly and review it with each daily review. If you need more space for any question, just grab a sheet of paper and keep writing.

1. What do you feel guilty about from the difficult experience? _____

   _____

   _____

2. Holding on to guilt can keep you stuck in the memory and feeling responsible for something you could not control. Are you ready to let the guilt go?

       YES   NO   I AM NOT SURE

   If you answered YES, then let it go. HINT: Deciding to let it go does not mean it is OK that it happened, just that you are deciding not to carry the guilt with you any longer.

   If you answered NO or I AM NOT SURE, what do you need to do to be ready to let the guilt go? When a situation turns out badly, we all wish we could have done something to have it turn out better.

3. What percentage was your responsibility? HINT: Only YOU can decide when to let the guilt go.

   _____

   _____

4. If you wish you had done something differently, why didn't you? What aspects of the difficult experience context impacted the choices you made at the time? Even if you were partly responsible for what happened, did anyone else also have some responsibility? _____

   _____

   _____

5. If your family member, loved one, or friend came to you to talk about feeling guilty about a difficult experience like what you went through, what would you say to them? _____

   _____

   _____

WORKSHEET 3.8: Exploring Emotions in Your Difficult Experience:

GUILT

Please choose which Exploring Emotions in Your Difficult Experience sheet/s (Worksheets 3.5 to 3.8) you want to review after each 20- to 30-minute difficult experience writing exercise (Worksheet 3.2) OR difficult experience daily review (Worksheet 3.4). Complete this worksheet once weekly and review it with each daily review. If you need more space for any question, just grab a sheet of paper and keep writing.

1. What do you feel guilty about from the difficult experience? _____

_____

_____

2. Holding on to guilt can keep you stuck in the memory and feeling responsible for something you could not control. Are you ready to let the guilt go?

      YES   NO   I AM NOT SURE

If you answered YES, then let it go. HINT: Deciding to let it go does not mean it is OK that it happened, just that you are deciding not to carry the guilt with you any longer.

If you answered NO or I AM NOT SURE, what do you need to do to be ready to let the guilt go? When a situation turns out badly, we all wish we could have done something to have it turn out better.

3. What percentage was your responsibility? HINT: Only YOU can decide when to let the guilt go.

_____

_____

4. If you wish you had done something differently, why didn't you? What aspects of the difficult experience context impacted the choices you made at the time? Even if you were partly responsible for what happened, did anyone else also have some responsibility? _____

_____

_____

5. If your family member, loved one, or friend came to you to talk about feeling guilty about a difficult experience like what you went through, what would you say to them? _____

_____

_____

WORKSHEET 3.8: Exploring Emotions in Your Difficult Experience:

GUILT

Please choose which Exploring Emotions in Your Difficult Experience sheet/s (Worksheets 3.5 to 3.8) you want to review after each 20- to 30-minute difficult experience writing exercise (Worksheet 3.2) OR difficult experience daily review (Worksheet 3.4). Complete this worksheet once weekly and review it with each daily review. If you need more space for any question, just grab a sheet of paper and keep writing.

1. What do you feel guilty about from the difficult experience? _____

    _____

    _____

2. Holding on to guilt can keep you stuck in the memory and feeling responsible for something you could not control. Are you ready to let the guilt go?

    YES   NO   I AM NOT SURE

    If you answered YES, then let it go. HINT: Deciding to let it go does not mean it is OK that it happened, just that you are deciding not to carry the guilt with you any longer.

    If you answered NO or I AM NOT SURE, what do you need to do to be ready to let the guilt go? When a situation turns out badly, we all wish we could have done something to have it turn out better.

3. What percentage was your responsibility? HINT: Only YOU can decide when to let the guilt go.

    _____

    _____

4. If you wish you had done something differently, why didn't you? What aspects of the difficult experience context impacted the choices you made at the time? Even if you were partly responsible for what happened, did anyone else also have some responsibility? _____

    _____

    _____

5. If your family member, loved one, or friend came to you to talk about feeling guilty about a difficult experience like what you went through, what would you say to them? _____

    _____

    _____

WORKSHEET 4.1: Your List of Daily Activities

Day	Activity
Monday	
Tuesday	
Wednesday	
Thursday	
Friday	
Saturday	
Sunday	

WORKSHEET 4.2: Your Action Plan

Week 1: Write down your goals for this coming week: _____

Day	Activity
Monday	
Tuesday	
Wednesday	
Thursday	
Friday	
Saturday	
Sunday	

Then, after you have done something on your list, evaluate it:

How did it go?

_____

How did you feel afterward?

_____

What do you want to try differently next time?

_____

Do you want to do this activity again?   _____Yes   _____No

What next?

_____

Week 2: Goals for this coming week: _____

Day	Activity
Monday	
Tuesday	
Wednesday	
Thursday	
Friday	
Saturday	
Sunday	

Week 3: Goals for this coming week: _____

Day	Activity
Monday	
Tuesday	
Wednesday	
Thursday	
Friday	
Saturday	
Sunday	

Week 4: Goals for this coming week: _____

Day	Activity
Monday	
Tuesday	
Wednesday	
Thursday	
Friday	
Saturday	
Sunday	

Week 5: Goals for this coming week: _____

Day	Activity
Monday	
Tuesday	
Wednesday	
Thursday	
Friday	
Saturday	
Sunday	

Week 6: Goals for this coming week: _____

Day	Activity
Monday	
Tuesday	
Wednesday	
Thursday	
Friday	
Saturday	
Sunday	

WORKSHEET 5.1: Social Connections Weekly Process and Planning

Social Connections   Week 1 Starting Date: _____

Who is one person you talked to this week? _____

How many times did you connect this week? _____

How long was the longest conversation? _____

Did you focus on: DIFFICULT EXPERIENCE _____   OTHER: _____

How did you feel after talking? **Rate yourself on the scale below:**

0---------1---------2---------3---------4---------5---------6---------7---------8---------9----------10
Better   Same   **Worse**

Note anything important about the contact: _____

After you have connected, consider how it went. Were you able to share your feelings? How did you feel afterward? What do you want to try differently next time? _____

_____

Do you want to repeat this social connection? If so, write down your plan for how to do that below. If not, plan an alternate social connection for next week. _____

_____

Social Connections   Week 2 Starting Date: _____

Who is one person you talked to this week? _____

How many times did you connect this week? _____

How long was the longest conversation? _____

Did you focus on: DIFFICULT EXPERIENCE _____   OTHER: _____

How did you feel after talking? **Rate yourself on the scale below:**

0---------1---------2---------3---------4---------5---------6---------7---------8---------9----------10
Better   Same   **Worse**

Social Connections   Week 3 Starting Date: _____

Who is one person you talked to this week? _____

How many times did you connect this week? _____

How long was the longest conversation? _____

Did you focus on: DIFFICULT EXPERIENCE _____   OTHER: _____

How did you feel after talking? Rate yourself on the scale below:

0---------1---------2---------3---------4---------5---------6---------7---------8---------9----------10
Better   Same   **Worse**

Social Connections   Week 4 Starting Date: _____

Who is one person you talked to this week? _____

How many times did you connect this week? _____

How long was the longest conversation? _____

Did you focus on: DIFFICULT EXPERIENCE _____   OTHER: _____

How did you feel after talking? Rate yourself on the scale below:

0---------1---------2---------3----------4----------5----------6----------7----------8----------9----------10
Better   **Same**   **Worse**

Social Connections   Week 5 Starting Date: _____

Who is one person you talked to this week? _____

How many times did you connect this week? _____

How long was the longest conversation? _____

Did you focus on: DIFFICULT EXPERIENCE _____   OTHER: _____

How did you feel after talking? Rate yourself on the scale below:

0---------1---------2---------3----------4----------5----------6----------7----------8----------9----------10
Better   **Same**   **Worse**

Social Connections   Week 6 Starting Date: _____

Who is one person you talked to this week? _____

How many times did you connect this week? _____

How long was the longest conversation? _____

Did you focus on: DIFFICULT EXPERIENCE _____   OTHER: _____

How did you feel after talking? Rate yourself on the scale below:

0---------1---------2---------3----------4----------5----------6----------7----------8----------9----------10
Better   **Same**   **Worse**

WORKSHEET 6.1: Healthy Eating Habits

Set a goal for yourself that is easy to achieve right away and do every day, such as reducing snacks, eating 1 serving of a vegetable or fresh fruit, cutting down on soda or caffeine, or making your lunch for work, and commit to this goal starting immediately. For some people, stress leads to eating more while others find that stress reduces their appetite. Consider how stress is impacting your eating habits and set a manageable goal for yourself. You can work through your goal using the worksheets in this workbook, and you can modify your goals from week to week.

Healthy Eating Goal for This Week: Please write your healthy eating goals on the lines below.

_____

_____

Sometimes it can help to have a partner working on healthy eating habits with you. This person can be an ally to talk with about the challenges of changing your eating, and you can give each other tips for how to succeed. If it is someone you live with, that's even better, as you can work together on healthy meals and having healthy snacks in your place.

Who could help you with your healthy eating habits this week? _____

ACTION PLAN FOR HEALTHY EATING NEXT WEEK

After you have worked on your eating habits for 1 week, think about how it went. How did you feel afterward?
_____

What do you want to try differently next week? _____

ACTION ASSESSMENT

Do you want to work on your eating habits again next week? Do you want to keep the same goals or try something different? _____

_____

ASSESSMENT

On the table below, write your weekly goal, check off the days that you completed your healthy eating habits goal, and write in any comments.

Day	Week 1 goal: ___	Week 2 goal: ___	Week 3 goal: ___	Week 4 goal: ___	Week 5 goal: ___	Week 6 goal: ___
Monday						
Tuesday						
Wednesday						
Thursday						
Friday						
Saturday						
Sunday						

WORKSHEET 6.2: Healthy Sleeping Habits

The aim of this exercise is getting enough sleep to feel rested. For most people that is 6 to 8 hours per night. Set a goal for yourself that is easy to achieve right away and every day, such as getting up when your alarm goes off rather than hitting the snooze button or going to sleep 15 minutes earlier each night, and commit to your goal starting immediately. You can work through your goal using the worksheets in this workbook. Please evaluate how your healthy sleeping action plan is going each week. Feel free to keep the same goals from week to week or change them.

Healthy Sleeping Goal for This Week:

_____

ACTION PLAN FOR HEALTHY SLEEPING NEXT WEEK

After you have worked on your sleep habits for 1 week, think about how it went. How did you feel afterward?

_____

What do you want to try differently next week? _____

ACTION ASSESSMENT

Do you want to work on your sleeping habits next week? Do you want to keep the same goals or try something different? _____

ASSESSMENT

On the table below, write your weekly goal, check off the days that you completed your healthy sleeping habits goal, and write in any comments.

Day	Week 1 goal: _____	Week 2 goal: _____	Week 3 goal: _____	Week 4 goal: _____	Week 5 goal: _____	Week 6 goal: _____
Monday						
Tuesday						
Wednesday						
Thursday						
Friday						
Saturday						
Sunday						

WORKSHEET 6.3: Healthy Exercise Habits

Set a goal for yourself that is easy to achieve right away and regularly, such as 10 minutes a day walking on your treadmill or riding on your exercise bike, and commit to starting it immediately. If you do not have exercise equipment, use what you do have access to, such as taking a walk outside or doing an online yoga class. You can work through your goal using the worksheets in this workbook. After a week of working on healthy exercise habits, evaluate how it went with the questions below. It is fine to keep the same goals from week to week or to modify them. If you are building up a new exercise habit, you may want to gradually increase the amount of time you exercise until you hit your target and then you can aim for that each time.

Healthy Exercise Goal for This Week:

_____

Sometimes it can help to invite a friend to exercise with you, especially if you exercise together. This person can be an ally to talk with about the challenges of starting a new exercise plan. You can even provide support and give each other tips for how to succeed.

Who would you like to invite to help with your exercise goal? _____

ACTION PLAN FOR HEALTHY EXERCISING NEXT WEEK
After you have worked on your exercise habits for one week, think about how it went. How did you feel afterward? _____

What do you want to try differently next week? _____

ACTION ASSESSMENT
Do you want to work on your exercise habits next week? Do you want to keep the same goals or try something different? _____

ASSESSMENT

On the table below, write your weekly goal, check off the days that you completed your healthy exercise habits goal, and write in any comments.

Day	Week 1 goal: _____	Week 2 goal: _____	Week 3 goal: _____	Week 4 goal: _____	Week 5 goal: _____	Week 6 goal: _____
Monday						
Tuesday						
Wednesday						
Thursday						
Friday						
Saturday						
Sunday						

WORKSHEET 6.4: Alcohol/Drugs and Self-Care

Set a goal for yourself that is easy to achieve right away and every day, such as limiting your alcohol to 1 drink per day or smoking pot only 3 days per week. After a week of working on this goal, evaluate how it went with the questions below. Feel free to keep the same goals from week to week or modify them.

Alcohol/Drug Goal for This Week:

_____

If you choose to drink alcohol or use drugs:

1. Use recreational alcohol and drugs in moderation.
2. Don't self-medicate with alcohol or drugs when you are stressed.
3. Don't self-medicate with drugs or alcohol to deal with the feelings you get when you think about difficult experiences.

ACTION PLAN FOR ALCOHOL/DRUGS AND SELF-CARE NEXT WEEK

After you worked on your use of alcohol and/or substances for a week, how did it go? How did you feel afterward? _____

What do you want to try differently next week? _____

ACTION ASSESSMENT

Do you want to work on your alcohol and/or drug use next week? Do you want to keep the same goals or try something different? _____

ASSESSMENT

On the table below, write your weekly goal, check off the days you hit your target for reducing alcohol and drug use, and write in any comments.

Day	Week 1 goal: ___	Week 2 goal: ___	Week 3 goal: ___	Week 4 goal: ___	Week 5 goal: ___	Week 6 goal: ___
Monday						
Tuesday						
Wednesday						
Thursday						
Friday						
Saturday						
Sunday						

Suggestions
for Pleasant Activities

Below is a list of activities that many people find pleasant to do. Mark ones that sound good to you. Please add other ideas wherever you like.

MOVEMENT

- ☐ Exercise
- ☐ Yoga/Stretch
- ☐ Rearrange your room or house
- ☐ Take a walk or hike
- ☐ Go for a bike ride
- ☐ Be outdoors
- ☐ See beautiful scenery
- ☐ [add your idea]:_____

SOCIALIZE

- ☐ Compliment/praise someone
- ☐ Talk about sports/current events
- ☐ Notice the good things that happen to family or friends

☐ Spend time with friends

☐ Reminisce, talk about old times

☐ Talk on the telephone

☐ Spend time with family

☐ Show an interest in what others say

☐ Plan or organize something

☐ Have friends come to visit (can be outside to be COVID-19 safe)

☐ Call an old friend

☐ Go to a meeting (book or other club, social group, AA or Al-Anon, or other)

☐ Make a new friend

☐ Go to a religious function

☐ Set up a Zoom or FaceTime call

☐ [add your idea]:_____

COMPASSION

☐ Consider one thing you are grateful for every day

☐ Brush someone else's hair

☐ Do volunteer work

☐ Send a card to someone who is sick

☐ Make food or crafts to give to a friend

☐ Plant flowers or buy a potted plant

☐ Help someone

☐ Pet/walk/groom your cat or dog

☐ Care for a houseplant

☐ Volunteer to help with an event or service activity

☐ [add your idea]:_____

COMFORT

☐ Take a long bath or shower; add Epsom salts, bubbles, fragrant bath oils

☐ Watch TV

☐ Eat a good meal

☐ Wear clothes you like

☐ Read a book

☐ Give yourself a manicure or pedicure

☐ Give yourself a facial

☐ [add your idea]:_____

FUN

- [ ] Go to a park, fair, or zoo
- [ ] Go to a garage sale
- [ ] Play a video game or app
- [ ] Do artwork or crafts
- [ ] Collect things
- [ ] Play cards or chess
- [ ] Go to a movie or play
- [ ] Go on an outing to the park, an event, etc.
- [ ] Go to a museum or exhibit
- [ ] Do a job well
- [ ] Learn to do something new
- [ ] Play a musical instrument
- [ ] [add your idea]:_____

SOUNDS

- [ ] Listen to music
- [ ] Listen to birds sing
- [ ] Sing
- [ ] Listen to the radio
- [ ] Listen to sounds of nature
- [ ] [add your idea]:_____

PRODUCTIVE/SELF-CARE

- [ ] Keep a clean house
- [ ] Solve a personal problem
- [ ] Do outdoor work
- [ ] Cook a good meal
- [ ] Get haircut/hair done
- [ ] [add your idea]:_____

READING/WRITING

- [ ] Go to the library
- [ ] Write letters
- [ ] Keep a journal

☐ Read the newspaper
☐ Write stories or poetry
☐ Read books or magazines
☐ Read something inspiring
☐ Read through old letters or journals
☐ Do crossword puzzles or play word games on your smart phone
☐ [add your idea]:_____

SIMPLE AND SILENT

☐ Say prayers
☐ Meditate or use mindful focus
☐ Sit in the sun
☐ Have peace and quiet
☐ Daydream
☐ Watch a sunset
☐ Watch people
☐ Look at clouds
☐ Look at old photograph
☐ Sit in a place of worship
☐ [add your idea]:_____

Additional Resources

EVIDENCE-BASED TREATMENT PROVIDERS

The following organizations have searchable provider database resources to connect with evidence-based treatment providers:

The International Society for Traumatic Stress Studies
http://www.istss.org/find-a-clinician.aspx

The Associate for Behavioral and Cognitive Therapies
http://www.findcbt.org/FAT/

The Anxiety and Depression Association of America
https://members.adaa.org/page/FATMain

The National Center for PTSD Website
https://www.ptsd.va.gov/gethelp/find_therapist.asp
(Note: even though this website is part of the US Department of Veterans' Affairs [VA], many VA therapists also have a private practice or they may be able to recommend a good trauma provider in the area.)

SUBSTANCE USE RESOURCES

Substance Abuse and Mental Health Services Administration (SAMHSA)
https://www.samhsa.gov/find-help/national-helpline
SAMHSA's National Helpline is a free, confidential, 24/7, 365-day-a-year treatment referral and information service (in English and Spanish) for individuals and families facing mental and/or substance use disorders.
Tel:1-800-662-4357
Also visit the online treatment locator:
https://findtreatment.samhsa.gov/

National Institute on Alcohol Abuse and Alcoholism, a Division of the National Institute of Health (NIH)—Treatment for Alcohol Problems: Finding and Getting Help
https://www.niaaa.nih.gov/publications/brochures-and-fact-sheets/treatment-alcohol-problems-finding-and-getting-help

National Institute on Alcohol Abuse and Alcoholism, a Division of the National Institute of Health (NIH)—Rethinking Drinking
https://www.rethinkingdrinking.niaaa.nih.gov/

Smart Recovery
https://www.smartrecovery.org/

Alcoholics Anonymous
https://www.aa.org/

Rethinking Drinking
https://www.rethinkingdrinking.niaaa.nih.gov/

POSTTRAUMATIC STRESS DISORDER (PTSD) AND MENTAL HEALTH RESOURCES

AboutFace and Make the Connection
https://www.ptsd.va.gov/apps/aboutface/
https://maketheconnection.net/resources#va-resources

AboutFace and Make the Connection are two sites presenting stories of veterans in their own words. The stories present military experiences as well as a wide range of treatment experiences and stories of recovery. The sites are intended to provide veterans in search of treatment with information to aid their own treatment decisions and encourage hope and help.

AboutFace is an online site developed by the National Center for PTSD in the Department of Veterans Affairs; it presents the stories of veterans who have survived trauma and then engaged in PTSD treatment. The stories are presented as videos of the veterans themselves and their family members. In these videos, they talk about the specifics of their PTSD and their treatment so that others can get familiar with what to expect and how treatment works. While the site is focused on military trauma, the stories are wide-ranging, with hundreds of veterans represented and discussing combat, military sexual trauma, and other traumas. While some of the content can be upsetting to hear, the stories of seeking care and getting help are encouraging and enlightening for those suffering with PTSD, their families, and the community at large. Since this is a VA-developed resource, the stories are focused on veterans, but many civilian trauma survivors have voiced similar experiences and stories. For instance, sexual trauma survivors tell us they can relate to the stories of military sexual trauma survivors who have been raped.

Similarly, the **Make the Connection** website (https://maketheconnection.net/conditions/ptsd) has the stories of many veterans and service members connecting to care for PTSD related to military and non-military traumas and other mental health issues.

Anxiety and Depression Association of America

https://adaa.org/understanding-anxiety/posttraumatic-stress-disorder-ptsd
The Anxiety and Depression Association of America website includes fact sheets and online information on reactions to trauma, PTSD, anxiety, depression, and treatment for people suffering with these problems and their families as well as professionals.

American Psychiatric Association

https://www.psychiatry.org/
The American Psychiatric Association is the national organization for psychiatrists, who generally prescribe medication for mental health conditions. The website contains information for patients and families.

American Psychiatric Association: PTSD

https://www.psychiatry.org/patients-families/ptsd/what-is-ptsd
The American Psychiatric Association PTSD page provides brief informational resources for patients and their families on the disorder, comorbid issues, and treatment options with emphasis on medical options for care.

American Psychological Association

https://www.apa.org/

The American Psychological Association is the national organization for psychologists, who generally provide psychotherapy for mental health conditions. The website contains information for patients and families.

American Psychological Association: PTSD

https://www.apa.org/topics/ptsd/

The American Psychological Association PTSD page provides brief informational resources for patients and their families on the disorder, comorbid issues, and treatment options including psychotherapy and medication options for treatment. The site includes information on how to choose a provider and support resources for caregivers of people suffering with PTSD.

Mental Health Care on the Military Heath System

http://afterdeployment.dcoe.mil/

The Mental Health Resources on the Military Health System website used to be hosted at AfterDeployment.org but now resides at http://afterdeployment.dcoe.mil/. This site has a wide variety of psychoeducational and self-help materials for issues that may arise in military personnel after deployment. While the primary focus is on military and veteran issues, many of the resources are also applicable to other people suffering with PTSD or other issues post-trauma, such as sleep difficulty, anger, or substance use.

National Crisis Line

https://suicidepreventionlifeline.org/

The National Crisis Line is a resource for people in crisis and their families focused on suicide prevention. The website has national resources for various crises that impact trauma survivors and people suffering with PTSD. A telephone service (988 or 1-800-273-8255), a text service, and online chat are available to call and talk to a person 24 hours a day.

National Alliance on Mental Illness (NAMI): PTSD

https://www.nami.org/Learn-More/Mental-Health-Conditions/Posttraumatic-Stress-Disorder/Support

The National Alliance on Mental Illness (NAMI) PTSD page covers basic information on the disorder for people suffering with PTSD and their families. In addition, it provides information on community resources for support for patients and their families.

National Center for PTSD

https://www.ptsd.va.gov/index.asp

The National Center for PTSD website has numerous resources for all audiences who may be interested in more information on the disorder, its treatment, and related conditions and issues. The site includes informational sheets, patient decision aids, and provider training.

National Child Traumatic Stress Network

https://www.nctsn.org/

The National Child Traumatic Stress Network provides information on trauma and stress in children, training for providers, psychoeducation for family, and treatment resources.

National Institute of Mental Health

https://www.nimh.nih.gov

The National Institute of Mental Health (NIMH) is the lead federal agency for research on mental disorders. Its website contains a wealth of information on numerous mental health disorders.

National Institute of Mental Health: PTSD

https://www.nimh.nih.gov/health/topics/post-traumatic-stress-disorder-ptsd/index.shtml

The National Institute of Mental Health PTSD page has numerous resources for all audiences who may be interested in more information on the disorder, its treatment, and related conditions and issues. The site includes informational sheets as well as ways to get involved in research.

Trauma-Focused Cognitive Behavioral Therapy (TF-CBT) Find a Therapist

https://tfcbt.org/therapists/

The TF-CBT is a first line evidence-based treatment for PTSD for use in children and adolescents with PTSD. The site includes links to find a therapist trained in trauma-focused cognitive behavioral therapy.

National Suicide Prevention Lifeline & Veterans Crisis Line

https://suicidepreventionlifeline.org/

https://www.Veteranscrisisline.net/get-help/local-resources

The National Suicide Prevention Lifeline is a resource for anyone in crisis or loved ones of people in crisis to be connected to resources and people to assist and help prevent suicide. This toll-free number (988 or 1-800-273-8255) includes a specific connection for veterans if they press 1 after dialing the main number. **988 has been designated as the new 3-digit dialing code for the National Suicide Prevention Lifeline and is available in all areas in the United States, starting July 16, 2022.** The Veterans Crisis Line is a resource for veterans in crisis and their families focused on suicide prevention. It is a part of the National Crisis Line specifically targeted to veterans. The website has national resources for various crises including those that impact trauma survivors and people suffering with PTSD, depression, anxiety disorder, substance abuse, or other issues. In addition, a crisis line provider is available to talk to a person 24 hours a day; a text service and online chat are also available.

WHAT ONLINE TOOLS ARE AVAILABLE?

While many online sites present themselves as though they have a magic cure, survivors of difficult or traumatic experiences should be cautious and do their best to make sure that the source of information is legitimate. Many people may be well-intentioned but not have a true understanding of the problem and the most effective treatments. Others are simply out to make money off people who are suffering. We encourage you to question any provider about their experience and use of evidence-based treatments. Be an informed consumer!

Some reputable resources online are described here.
The National Alliance on Mental Illness (NAMI; https://www.nami.org/Learn-More/Mental-Health-Conditions/Posttraumatic-Stress-Disorder/Support) has many online resources to connect someone suffering with PTSD or their family to information, crisis intervention, and clinical treatment resources.

Similarly, the **National Institute of Mental Health** (https://www.helpguide.org/articles/ptsd-trauma/ptsd-symptoms-self-help-treatment.htm/) has information and resources for those suffering with PTSD from all types of trauma.

The **National Center for PTSD** website (https://www.ptsd.va.gov/) includes many resources for survivors and their family and friends to learn about deployment, trauma, PTSD, and its treatment. The resources range from written materials on the latest research findings about the development and treatment of PTSD to online videos and whiteboard videos about how treatment works or how to access care. While these often focus on veterans and military, other types of trauma, such as sexual assault and child abuse, are also represented.

Another resource developed for military service members and veterans is **Afterdeployment.org** (https://www.afterdeployment.org/). This site offers education as well as some focused online treatment resources for military service members and their families following deployment. As with **AboutFace**, some of these resources for PTSD are also relevant to nonmilitary trauma survivors.

ARE THERE USEFUL APPS?

In addition to the online information about PTSD and PTSD treatment, some specific apps are useful for people following difficult experiences and their families. Many of these apps were developed by the VA and the Department of Defense but were created for use by people who have survived many different types of trauma, not just military-related experiences.

Messy Memories (available on the app store) is very similar to the program presented in this workbook and may be useful in conjunction with the *Making Meaning of Difficult Experiences* workbook. This app allows you to audio record the memory of the difficult experience and listen to it repeatedly.

Veterans Affairs Mental Health App Store (https://mobile.va.gov/appstore/mental-health) has a number of apps that focus on mental health issues, coping, and treatment. Some are designed for use while working with a therapist and others are set up to walk you through coping resources on your own. All are free of charge for download.

COVID Coach (https://mobile.va.gov/app/covid-coach) is an app developed by the Department of Veterans Affairs as a general self-help app for use during the COVID-19 pandemic. It includes self-assessment and several modules that you can review and use to cope with stress related to the pandemic.

Another app, the **CBT-I Coach** (https://mobile.va.gov/app/cbt-i-coach), may be useful for those suffering from primary insomnia who may be working through CBT for insomnia (CBT-I) with a mental health professional. This app provides a convenient way to record sleep and sleep quality as well as tools to assist with sleep restriction and psychoeducation on sleep hygiene.

CPT Coach (https://mobile.va.gov/app/cpt-coach) is an app intended for use while working with a therapist in CPT. The app provides many of the forms for cognitive restructuring and psychoeducational materials explaining why the treatment works.

PE Coach (https://mobile.va.gov/app/pe-coach-2) is an app that is intended for use while working with a therapist in prolonged exposure (PE) therapy. This app can assist with secure recording of the trauma memory that is part of this treatment as well as planning for practice exercises and recording of distress ratings as the trauma survivor works through the exposures in PE to take their life back from PTSD. Both apps (CPT Coach and PE Coach) are intended to be used while in treatment with a PE or CPT provider and not as self-help treatments. Several other apps for use in therapy are also available through the VA app site (https://mobile.va.gov/appstore).

PTSD Coach (https://mobile.va.gov/app/ptsd-coach) is an app designed for coping with the symptoms of PTSD. It is not a treatment, but many people suffering with PTSD have found it helpful to use prior to treatment or even after treatment to maintain gains and explore new ways to cope with anxiety and stress as well as PTSD.

INDEX

AboutFace, 192–193, 196

Afterdeployment.org, 194, 196

Alcoholics Anonymous (AA), 114, 192

alcohol
    action plan, 95–96
    Ann (case example), 15, 25, 85, 105
    cognitive behavioral therapy, 114
    David (case example), 62, 85–86, 106
    getting help, 90, 111, 114, 192
    healthy habits, 95–96
    Miguel (case example), 15, 107
    recommended consumption limits, 95
    self-care assessment, 89
    Shaquila (case example), 87
    sleep hygiene and, 92
    tips for, 95
    Worksheet 6.4: Alcohol/Drugs and
        Self-Care, 103–104, 184–185

American Psychiatric Association, 193

American Psychological Association,
    193–194

anger
    Ann (case example), 26, 29
    being "stuck" in, 9, 15, 26
    David (case example), 106
    Miguel (case example), 15, 62
    as response to trauma, 11, 14
    Worksheet 3.7: Exploring Emotions in Your
        Difficult Experience: Anger, 33, 37–38,
        46, 160–165

Ann (sexual assault case example)
    avoidance, 15, 17, 25–26, 61
    Getting Active skill, 61, 75, 87,
        105–106
    introduction to, 6, 13
    Memory Exposure and Processing
        skill, 21–22, 25, 28–29, 105–106
    Self-Care skill, 85, 105–106
    Social Connection skill, 75, 105–106

anxiety
    anxiety disorders, 5, 111–112, 195
    cognitive behavioral therapy, 113
    getting help, 16, 111–113, 191, 193, 195, 197
    negative self-statements, 19
    processing difficult experience
        memories, 16, 18
    prolonged exposure therapy, 16
    Worksheet 3.6: Exploring Emotions in Your
        Difficult Experience: Fear or Anxiety, 33,
        37–38, 45, 154–159

Anxiety and Depression Association of
America, 191, 193
Association for Behavioral and Cognitive
Therapies, 191
avoidance. *See also* isolation
Ann (case example), 15, 17, 25–26, 61
Helen (case example), 20
of memories and reminders, 5–6, 9, 15–17,
20, 25–26, 30–31, 76, 108–109
Miguel (case example), 14, 62
processing memory related to, 30
of realistically safe situations, 18, 20, 114

behavioral activation, 9, 61–74. *See also*
Getting Active skill
accountability, 63–64
assessment of self-care, 64–65
being kind and forgiving with yourself, 66
breaking activities down into smaller
steps, 66
examples of self-care activities, 63–64
inertia, 63
inviting friend to participate, 66
monitoring, 67
overview of, 9, 63
planning, 65
review of, 109
tips for, 67
tracking, 64–65
blame. *See* guilt

case examples. *See* Ann (sexual assault case
example); David (pandemic case
example); Helen (traffic accident case
example); Miguel (combat case example);
Shaquila (miscarriage case example)
CBT-I Coach, 197
checking in with yourself, 27–28, 79–80,
108

clinical nurse specialists (CNSs), 113
cognitive behavioral therapy (CBT), 111,
113–114, 191, 195, 197
cognitive processing therapy (CPT), 114, 197
cognitive restructuring, 114, 197
combat and military trauma, 2. *See also* Miguel
(combat case example)
couples counseling, 114
COVID Coach, 197
COVID-19 pandemic, 1–2. *See also* David
(pandemic case example)
deciding when memories begin and end, 30
helping others but neglecting self, 23
not wanting to forget, 22
self-care during, 63
social isolation, 10
struggles arising as the result of, 2
CPT (cognitive processing therapy), 114, 197
CPT Coach, 197

David (pandemic case example)
avoidance and isolation, 15, 26
Getting Active skill, 62–65, 75–76, 106
guilt, 17
helping others but neglecting self, 23
introduction to, 6–7, 14–15
Memory Exposure and Processing skill,
25–26, 48–60, 106
not wanting to forget, 22
Self-Care skill, 85–87, 106
Social Connection skill, 75–76, 81, 106
death of loved ones, 1–2, 16. *See also* David
(pandemic case example); Miguel
(combat case example); Shaquila (miscarriage case example)
depression, 5, 107, 109
David (case example), 76
exercise and, 94
getting help, 111–114, 191, 193, 195

Miguel (example), 62
negative self-statements, 19
Shaquila (case example), 8
discrimination, 115
divorce, 1–2
drugs, 13, 15
    action plan, 95–96
    Ann (case example), 13, 21, 25, 29, 85, 105
    cognitive behavioral therapy, 114
    getting help, 90, 111–112, 114, 192,
        194–195
    healthy habits, 95–96
    negative social connections, 77
    self-care assessment, 90
    substance use disorders, 5, 112, 114
    Worksheet 6.4: Alcohol/Drugs and Self-
        Care, 103–104, 110, 184–185

EAPs (employee assistance programs), 11, 114
eating
    action plan, 91
    Ann (case example), 105–106
    David (case example), 7, 25, 62, 86–87, 106
    self-care, 10, 87–88, 91
    Shaquila (case example), 8, 68, 87
    sleep hygiene and, 92
    Worksheet 6.1: Healthy Eating Habits, 86,
        97–98, 178–179
EMDR (eye movement desensitization and
    reprocessing), 114
emotions. *See also* anger; fear; guilt; Memory
    Exposure and Processing skill; processing
    difficult experience memories; sadness
    combination of positive and negative, 37
    exploring emotions connected to difficult
        experience, 37
    fight, flee, or freeze, 29
    focusing on, 35–36
    hard-wired for, 29

    intensity in relation to experience and
        length of time since, 37
    letting yourself feel, 31–32
    not dangerous, good, or bad, 28–29
    really feeling, 30
    riding wave of, 28, 35
    tracking, 28–29
employee assistance programs (EAPs), 11, 114
enjoyable activities
    assessment of self-care, 90
    behavioral activation, 63
    suggestions for, 187–190
exercise
    action plan, 94–95
    amount and types of, 94
    Ann (case example), 61, 75, 85, 105
    David (case example), 7, 62, 64, 85–86, 106
    healthy habits, 94–95
    self-care, 10, 89
    Shaquila (case example), 87
    sleep hygiene and, 92
    tips for, 94
    Worksheet 6.3: Healthy Exercise Habits,
        101–102, 182–183
eye movement desensitization and
    reprocessing (EMDR), 114

family counseling, 114
fear
    being "stuck" in, 9, 15, 26
    getting help, 16, 111
    Helen (case example), 19
    Worksheet 3.6: Exploring Emotions in Your
        Difficult Experience: Fear or Anxiety, 33,
        37–38, 45, 154–159

gender-based trauma, 1–2, 115
Getting Active skill, 61–74
    accountability, 63–64

Getting Active skill (*cont.*)
   assessment of self-care, 64–65
   behavioral activation, 9, 63
   being kind and forgiving with yourself, 66
   breaking activities down into smaller steps, 66
   David (case example), 62–65
   defined, 63
   examples of self-care activities, 63–64
   inertia, 63
   inviting friend to participate, 66
   Miguel (case example), 67
   monitoring, 67
   overview of, 9
   planning activities, 65
   review of, 109
   Shaquila (case example), 67–70
   tips for, 67
   tracking activities, 64–65
   Worksheet 4.1: Your List of Daily Activities,
      64, 71, 109, 172
   Worksheet 4.2: Your Action Plan, 65–66,
      69–70, 72–74, 109, 173–175
grief process, 16–17
guilt
   Ann (case example), 13, 17, 22, 75, 105–106
   avoidance and isolation, 10, 37, 76, 109
   being "stuck" in, 26
   David (case example), 17
   getting help, 111
   Miguel (case example), 15, 22, 26, 62
   self-blame, 13–15, 17, 22, 26
   social support, 78
   Worksheet 3.8: Exploring Emotions in Your
      Difficult Experience: Guilt, 33, 37–38,
      47, 166–171

hate crimes, 2
Helen (traffic accident case example)
   early intervention, 18–20, 107

follow up assessments, 20
   introduction to, 7, 14–15
hypervigilance, 14–15

International Society for Traumatic Stress
      Studies, 191
interpersonal violence, 2
isolation, 10, 14–17, 109. *See also* avoidance;
      Social Connection skill
   Ann (case example), 17, 61
   David (case example), 6, 15, 62
   Miguel (case example), 15, 67
   Shaquila (case example), 8, 26

job loss, 1

Make the Connection, 192–193
memories. *See also* Memory Exposure and
      Processing skill
   avoiding, 5–6, 9, 15–17, 20, 25–26, 108–109
   being "stuck" or trapped in, 5–6, 8, 15,
      26, 37–38
   deciding beginning and ending of, 30
   deciding which to process first, 30–32
   emotionally processing (working through),
      5–6, 9, 16–23, 34–38, 108–109
   "erasing," 21
   not wanting to forget, 22
   taking over your life, 22–23
Memory Exposure and Processing skill, 25–38
   baseline score, 28
   checking in with yourself, 27–28
   David (case example), 48–60
   deciding when memories begin and end, 30
   deciding which memory to process first, 30
   emotions are not dangerous, good, or
      bad, 28–29
   learning to process difficult
      experiences, 30–33

as new skill, 38

overview of, 9

processing difficult experience
memories, 34–38

review of, 108–109

Worksheet 3.1: Mood Thermometers, 28–30,
39, 49, 54, 59, 108, 118–123

Worksheet 3.2: Difficult Experience Writing
Exercise, 31–34, 40–41, 50, 55, 108, 124–135

Worksheet 3.3: Difficult Experience
Processing Exercise, 33, 36, 42, 51, 56,
108, 136–141

Worksheet 3.4: Daily Review of the Difficult
Experience Writing Exercise, 32–34, 43,
53, 57, 142–147

Worksheet 3.5: Exploring Emotions in Your
Difficult Experience: Sadness, 33, 37–38,
44, 52, 58, 148–153

Worksheet 3.6: Exploring Emotions in Your
Difficult Experience: Fear or Anxiety, 33,
37–38, 45, 154–159

Worksheet 3.7: Exploring Emotions in Your
Difficult Experience: Anger, 33, 37–38,
46, 160–165

Worksheet 3.8: Exploring Emotions in Your
Difficult Experience: Guilt, 33, 37–38,
47, 166–171

writing/recording about difficult experience
memories, 31–34

Messy Memories app, 2, 9, 27, 196

microaggressions, 1

Miguel (combat case example)

Getting Active skill, 62, 67, 76

introduction to, 7, 14–15

Memory Exposure and Processing skill, 26,
30, 107

not wanting to forget, 22

Self-Care skill, 87, 107

Social Connection skill, 75–76, 107

Military Heath System, 194

miscarriage, 2. *See also* Shaquila (miscarriage
case example)

Narcotics Anonymous (NA), 114

National Alliance on Mental Illness (NAMI),
114, 194, 196

National Center for PTSD, 191–192,
194, 196

National Child Traumatic Stress Network, 194

National Crisis Line, 194–195

National Institute of Mental Health, 195–196

National Institute on Alcohol Abuse and
Alcoholism, 90, 192

National Suicide Prevention Lifeline, 11, 27,
112, 195

natural disasters, 1–2, 23

natural recovery, 20

nurse practitioners, 113

PAs (physician assistants), 113

PE (prolonged exposure) therapy, 16, 62, 87,
107, 111, 114, 197

PE Coach, 197

physical assault, 1–2

physician assistants (PAs), 113

"pink elephant" example, 5

pleasant (enjoyable) activities

assessment of self-care, 90

behavioral activation, 63

suggestions for, 187–190

posttraumatic growth, 21, 108

posttraumatic stress disorder (PTSD), 5–6. *See
also* Miguel (combat case example)

early intervention, 18

exercise and, 94

getting help, 16, 18, 111–114, 191–197

Helen (case example), 18, 20

natural recovery, 20

processing difficult experience memories,
    5–6, 9, 16–23, 34–38, 108–109. *See also*
    Memory Exposure and Processing skill
  celebrating success in approaching the
    memory, 36
  defined, 26–27
  exploring emotions connected to experi-
    ence, 37
  focusing on emotions, 35–36
  meaning of the memory, 36–37
  not rushing, 35
  not trying to fix, 35–36
  rating level of distress, 34
  remembering details, 35
  rumination, 35–36
  sticking with the work, 35
  thinking about how approaching the
    memory went, 36
  varying patterns of distress and pro-
    cessing, 34–35
professional help, 11, 110–115
  alcohol and drugs, 90, 111
  finding providers, 112, 191–195
  knowing when to ask for, 111–112
  no shame in, 111
  online tools, 195–197
  types of providers, 113
  types of therapies and programs, 112–115
prolonged exposure (PE) therapy, 16, 62, 87,
    107, 111, 114, 197
psychiatrists, 113
psychologists, 113
psychotherapy (talk therapy), 112–113
PsyPact, 113
PTSD. *See* posttraumatic stress disorder
PTSD Coach, 197

race-based trauma, 1–2, 115
resilience, 1, 26, 28, 108–112

  Ann (case example), 85
  David (case example), 106
  posttraumatic growth, 21, 108
Rethinking Drinking, 90, 192
rumination, 35–36

sadness
  Ann (case example), 29
  behavioral activation, 63
  being "stuck" in, 9, 15, 26
  David (case example), 52, 58, 60
  death of loved ones, 35, 37
  getting help, 16, 111
  Miguel (case example), 62
  Shaquila (case example), 67–68
  Worksheet 3.5: Exploring Emotions in Your
    Difficult Experience: Sadness, 33, 37–38,
    44, 52, 58, 148–153
SAMHSA (Substance Abuse and Mental
    Health Services Administration), 192
Self-Care skill, 85–104
  action plans, 91–96
  assessment of self-care, 88–90
  Helen (case example), 19
  helping others but neglecting self, 23
  overview of, 10
  reasons for neglecting self-care, 87–88
  review of, 110
  types of self-care activities, 87, 187–190
  Worksheet 6.1: Healthy Eating Habits, 97–
    98, 110, 178–179
  Worksheet 6.2: Healthy Sleeping Habits,
    99–100, 110, 180–181
  Worksheet 6.3: Healthy Exercise Habits,
    101–102, 110, 182–183
  Worksheet 6.4: Alcohol/Drugs and Self-
    Care, 86, 103–104, 110, 184–185
self-statements, 19
serious illness, 1

sexual assault, 1–2. *See also* Ann (sexual assault case example)

sexual harassment, 1

Shaquila (miscarriage case example)

 Getting Active skill, 67–70

 introduction to, 8

 Memory Exposure and Processing skill, 26, 107

 Self-Care skill, 87

sleep, 14–15

 action plan, 91–94

 Ann (case example), 13

 clocks, 92

 David (case example), 7, 14, 60, 62

 electronics, 93

 getting help, 111, 114, 194, 197

 healthy habits, 91–94

 insomnia, 92

 Miguel (case example), 15, 87, 107

 naps, 93

 self-care assessment, 88

 sleep hygiene, 91–93

 standardizing routing, 92–93

 stimulants, 92

 tips for processing, 93

 Worksheet 6.2: Healthy Sleeping Habits, 99–100, 180–181

Smart Recovery, 192

Social Connection skill, 75–84

 adding connections, 82

 allowing time for connections, 80

 carefully considering who can help, 78–79

 checking in with yourself, 79–80

 focus on listening rather than fixing, 77–78

 goals of, 82

 making plan to connect, 80

 meaningful conversation, 80

 need for social connections, 76

 negative social connections, 77

 overview of, 10

 positive social connections, 77–78

 reaching out for social support, 76–77

 review of, 109–110

 sharing "versions" of story with different connections, 78

 talking until you don't need to anymore, 79

 telling your story, 79

 tips for, 80

 Worksheet 5.1: Social Connections Weekly Process and Planning, 80–84, 110, 176–177

social workers, 113

Substance Abuse and Mental Health Services Administration (SAMHSA), 192

substance use. *See* alcohol; drugs

suicidal ideation, 11, 112, 195

talk therapy (psychotherapy), 112–113

traffic accidents, 1–2. *See also* Helen (traffic accident case example)

Trauma-Focused Cognitive Behavioral Therapy (TF-CBT), 195

traumatic experiences

 approaching and revisiting memories, 16–22

 asking for help, 110–115

 being "stuck" or trapped in memory of, 5–6, 8, 15, 26, 37–38

 defined, 15–16

 early intervention, 18

 effects of, 5, 8

 emotionally processing (working through), 5–6, 9, 15, 17–18, 22–23

 lack of improvement, 11

 memories taking over your life, 22–23

 natural recovery, 20

 not wanting to forget, 22

 number of adults who will experience, 2

traumatic experiences (*cont.*)
   posttraumatic growth, 21, 108
   purpose of workbook and program, 1–2, 8
   skills involved in program, 9–10
   using workbook, 2–3, 10
   when to expect to see improvement, 3

US Department of Veterans' Affairs (VA),
      191–193, 196–197

Veterans Affairs Mental Health App Store, 196
Veterans Crisis Line, 195

worksheets
   3.1 Mood Thermometers, 28–30, 39, 49, 54,
      59, 108, 118–123
   3.2 Difficult Experience Writing Exercise,
      31–34, 40–41, 50, 55, 108, 124–135
   3.3 Difficult Experience Processing
      Exercise, 33, 36, 42, 51, 56, 108, 136–141
   3.4 Daily Review of the Difficult Experience
      Writing Exercise, 32–34, 43, 53, 57,
      142–147
   3.5 Exploring Emotions in Your Difficult
      Experience: Sadness, 33, 37–38, 44, 52,
      58, 148–153
   3.6 Exploring Emotions in Your Difficult
      Experience: Fear or Anxiety, 33, 37–38,
      45, 154–159
   3.7 Exploring Emotions in Your Difficult
      Experience: Anger, 33, 37–38, 46,
      160–165

   3.8 Exploring Emotions in Your Difficult
      Experience: Guilt, 33, 37–38, 47,
      166–171
   4.1 Your List of Daily Activities, 64, 71,
      109, 172
   4.2 Your Action Plan, 65–66, 69–70, 72–74,
      109, 173–175
   5.1 Social Connections Weekly Process and
      Planning, 80–84, 110, 176–177
   6.1 Healthy Eating Habits, 86, 97–98, 110,
      178–179
   6.2 Healthy Sleeping Habits, 99–100, 110,
      180–181
   6.3 Healthy Exercise Habits, 86, 101–102,
      110, 182–183
   6.4 Alcohol/Drugs and Self-Care, 86, 103–104,
      110, 184–185
   using, 2–3, 10, 27
writing/recording about difficult experience
      memories, 31–34. *See also* Memory
      Exposure and Processing skill
   choosing time for, 32
   deciding when memories begin and end, 32
   describing memories in present tense, 31
   going through memories three times, 32, 34
   including all details, 31–32
   keeping workbook in safe place, 31
   letting yourself feel emotions, 31–32
   rereading daily, 34
   rewriting weekly, 34
   tips for processing, 32–33
   tips for recounting memories, 31